www.Oracleilluminated.com

Want to join the Illuminators and submit your coloring images to the illumination gallery?

The Illuminators are colorists of Oracle Illuminated coloring book images. We are very excited to see your beautiful creations and experience this creative collaboration with you. We encourage you to share your coloring images, thoughts, emotions and comments about the experience.

Send submissions to Oracleilluminated@gmail.com

* Name, location, and comment submissions are encouraged, yet optional.

Visit the Illumination Gallery to view the beautiful coloring images of the Illuminators!

https://www.oracleilluminated.com/illuminators/

Follow 👁 **Share**
Instagram: **Oracle Illuminated**
Facebook: **Oracle Illuminated**
Pinterest: **Oracle Illuminated**

NOTICE!

Hello Friends,

Normally when one of my patrons has bought one of my works of Art, I like to send them a hand written thank you note. With this book however, it is not realistic to send each of you a note so I am including this one at the beginning of the book to tell you all how eternally grateful I am.

I hope that those of you who have purchased this book or received it as a gift take the time to let the work speak to you. Trust me, it will in many ways. I am super excited to hear from you and see your amazing coloring images. I also understand there might be those of you who don't resonate with this work but believe you me you purchased it or acquired it by no mistake. Take what resonates and pass the book along to a friend, a coffee shop, or even a thrift shop so someone else can find use in it. A huge thankyou in advance for doing so!

Truly this is a gift to my life to be able to collaborate with each of you through this coloring book. I want to extend to each of you a heartfelt thank you for your support of the first Art of a multi-phase project of metaphysical coloring books and oracle card decks. I have forty-four more archetypes for Visions Illuminated Vol. 2 and Vol. 3 coming soon so be on the lookout for the rest of the Visions Illuminated Coloring book series. And sometime after the release of vol. 3 we will begin work on the Visions Illuminated oracle card Deck!
Much love, may your visions be Illuminated.
Julia Luke XXOO

About the Author

Hello friends! My name is Julia Luke and I am a psychic medium and an intuitive artist from Tacoma, Washington. I have been creating art since early childhood, but really started to channel art unconsciously in my early twenties after a severe car accident that resulted in a near death experience(NDE). The car crash and NDE was a turning point in my life, and it's when I began to create art through trance channeling which I experienced as an intense sense of peace and love which gave meaning to my life when previously I was aimless.

Since that life-changing event, I have pursued art full time with an inner calling toward the path as a channel of spirit through my art, council, and readings. As a creative mystic, an empathic healer, and a messenger between worlds I have walked the path of abuse, dysfunction and painful life experiences as initiations that guided me inwards to hear my own soul during the darkest of hours of my life. I have been creating therapeutic, intuitive, and psychic art for seventeen years, reading oracle and tarot cards for over ten years, and giving psychic medium readings for eight years.

I deliver messages and energy in my art as it comes to me. Each type of art medium will change how it appears and how it feels which is why mixed media is my favorite method of creating art. I feel like a variety of tools gives me the most freedom to express the diversity of what I am tuning into and receiving energetically. I have many styles of creating which facilitate exploration of the unknown. The variety of creative tools mimic how I use my Clair Senses to communicate with spirit, including clairvoyance (clear seeing), clairaudience (clear hearing), clairsentience-empathic (clear feeling), claircognizant (clear knowing), clairscent (clear smelling), and channeling.

There is a perception that if you are a psychic medium and in tuned with spirit, your artwork should look a certain way, which tends to acknowledge the light yet dismiss the teaching of the darker aspects of life which have no judgment from spirit. Spirit honors freewill and the lessons of growth it gives us in life. Without the dark we could not value the light. Editing out the negative lessons in life is limiting oneself from learning, growing, and experiencing the rich consciousness of oneself. By not loving both the light and dark aspects of oneself unconditionally, you are not honoring your own free choice and the vast creative expression of the universal consciousness that created us.

My artwork is encoded with seeds of heart-consciousness that remind all the souls that are drawn to my channelings that they are loved by the creative source of the universe. These seeds help remind your hearts that you are indeed birthed from love. You are magnificent creators worthy of believing in yourself, loving yourself, and being your true self. I am a mirroring empath, if you listen to the whisperings of my archetypes it will give you guidance in many subtle and direct ways, known and unknown, and given with love.

Julia Luke

Preface

The Visions Illuminated Coloring Books came to me through a series of visions and promptings. The title of the brand and books mirror the fact I am illuminating visions that I have as a psychic medium and intuitive artist. The Visions Illuminated Coloring Books came about through visions from two separate timelines. First in 2008, I had two visions that came to me, the first was creating coloring books and the second was to create my own tarot and oracle card decks. At that time, I was preoccupied with creating for art shows and galleries. I knew intuitively these were meant for a future date, so I made a mental note of the visions and put them on my creative shelf for safe keeping.

Fast forward to the fall of 2015, I had been a professional artist for nine years and had over fifty shows under my belt. I had plenty of amazing experiences with art exhibition but my desire for showing in galleries had dampened at that point. I felt that gallery work had a ceiling and I wanted to expand further as a creator. I had a prompting and a vision to create an oracle card deck and began work channeling those images. I heard my inner being say to me if I was going to illustrate the images I could offer the base sketches as coloring books first then illustrate them as my card deck and it fit energetically. It felt fun, felt expansive, felt right, so I said YES!

In March of 2016 I started creating the first images for the archetypes. I was instructed intuitively to write a list of titles and not consecutively create from the list but to channel the art as it came. So, when each archetype was finished as a channeled drawing, I would look at the list and gauge each title by its energy to determine which title fit with the archetype I had created. Without fail the match always vibrated with high energy to indicate it was its counterpart. This type of process is not too far off from how I created my art before this project. I always channeled the art, finished and then decoded its message, and then the title came to me last.

The physical process to the art was a lot of work, yet I do love channeling, so I will do what is required to get the job done. What was challenging to me is I am accustomed to working with a lot of art at once. I would rotate between paintings, always having my hand in several pies at once. However, this project came through with a devoted step by step process.

Each image had to be hand drawn three times in a specific series of steps. First, the base sketch with pencil on tracing paper. Second, I would flip the image over onto bristol paper and transfer the image. Third, I would then ink the image then repeat. By late summer of 2016 I had finished thirty-three images and was going to release the first book by that fall, but I got another prompting to do eleven more and split the books into two volumes of twenty-two archetypes each. So, I trusted my intuition and began to bring eleven more archetypes though. By that fall, I was finished with the art and started to channel the written component to the archetypes, hoping I would be able to release the books by early 2017. Another prompting then came to also put out a sister book to each regular volume released as midnight edition consisting of black filled patterns, so I could offer a variation of coloring levels to the market.

January of 2017 came, and my husband and I decided to sell our home and down size, so we could prioritize and have less distractions from the creative projects we were both working on. I had to put the project on hold which to be honest, I really needed a break. Around early summer, I had finished the writing for the archetypes and realized I needed a new computer at that time. I had a 9-year-old dinosaur of a laptop that was constantly overheating but you make do with what you have. For this project I knew I was going to have to upgrade to get the quality I needed to finish the digital details. I found a beautiful computer that was way out of my budget, but it was made for artists and I felt it was made for me. I put out to the universe my gratitude for that computer and a few months later it arrived by synchronistic funding and some pretty magical events. With absolute knowing in my heart that I was supported by the universe I ecstatically resumed the project.

By winter of 2017 I was working on the last details before publishing. I got another vision prompting me to add twenty-two more images to the back of the book consisting of energetically coded seamless patterns and mandalas. I listened and added twenty-two more images for trance and meditative coloring. I'll be honest, at that point I was more than ready to launch this project since it was creeping up on two years since I had started. I had faith since everything I needed for this to come together was guided from my higher-self. I had to trust that there was a reason for it being created at the pace it was and that I was to remain faithful regardless of the time it took.

My archetypes and oracle images are divinely guided to help stimulate messages from the subconscious of those who view it. It can unnerve you and create anxiety, or make you feel magic and a deep curious love, but regardless of the emotions that stir within you, try to understand "why?" Why does the art evoke this in me? Is it just the art and the artist's energy? Or is it what you are projecting at it? Or all the above? There is no right or wrong answer from my side of the work. I will leave that truth up to you as the viewer. I am the messenger to deliver it for you to discover. Do know these images have messages for you. I suggest being open to receiving its guidance in known and unknown ways.

I love creative collaboratives and have done many with artists which I enjoyed tremendously but wanted to find a way I could expand and reach people who did not self-identify as a professional artist. This project is a way to share and collaborate with the masses. I am so excited to see how the art speaks to you and how it wants to be expressed through you. When I channel art, I ask each piece, "How would you like to come through?", and then I trust moment by moment as it expresses its essence through me.

While channeling and creating this project I experienced many emotions, experiences, and energy of each archetype in my own life. Each time I worked with an archetype's expression, I energetically became very familiar with it and its energy signature. The one important thing here I want to illuminate is that I created this being both true to myself and to my love of creation. When I create, it brings absolute freedom and peace which is divinely guided with love and encouragement.

My work is a provocative mystical experience designed for colorists looking for more to explore. I want to thank all of you who supported this venture and helped a long-awaited date with destiny come to fruition. I also want to thank all the people, clients, patrons, friends who believed in me and supported me along the way. Last but not least a huge thank you to my husband Jason for editing these books and believing in this project, loving me and supporting me wholeheartedly.

Julia Luke

Tips & Tricks

- To remove your pages cleanly without tearing the pages, X-ACTO Knifes or a utility knife deliver the sharpest, most accurate cut. Cut the page close to the spine and slowly cut with slight pressure. Do take caution that if you cut too deeply it can cut other pages beneath it.

- I do give permission to take the images out of the book and make copies for personal coloring use only. I promote the exploration of practice coloring several variations of the same image. You can color them digitally or print the images onto a thicker paper such as card stock for wet media such as acrylic and watercolor. For all other uses rights are reserved ® Oracle Illuminated.

- To protect the pages beneath your coloring image while using wet media like markers always use a separate piece of paper to put underneath your coloring image. I suggest a few sheets of printer paper or a single sheet of card stock.

- What types of tools to color with? You can use a variety of mediums to color with, but I suggest for Visions Illuminated Coloring Book paper to use colored pencils, graphite, pencils, ink pens, gel pens, **solvent-based markers** and soft pastels. *Crayons work as well but can be harder to get into smaller details if you're looking for precision coloring. **Water-based markers** tend to saturate the paper which can lead to tearing/excessive bleeding.

- If you are using colored pencils keep your pencils sharpened frequently.

- To keep track of the colors you have used for a coloring image I suggest writing down the colors if they have a color code, keeping a separate container for tools in use or making your own color chart and numbering the markers or colored pencils at the bottom with a permanent marker if they do not have a manufacturer color code.

- Try using mixed media such as coloring the image with colored pencils, after a good layer of wax is built up you can then use water-based markers to saturate the color over the colored pencil areas and blend out with a Q-tip or paper stump. You can get some great shading and brighter colors that really pop! *Avoid using water-based markers without that wax layer!

- Try using a paper stump, and odorless mineral spirits, also known as Terpenoid, with your colored pencils for blending. I do suggest testing solvent products on a separate piece of paper to see how they work with your pencils before applying them to your image. Remember to let go and let your inner child come through and play. Creative play and coloring is not about perfection it's about exploration. Relax and have fun my friends! Happy coloring and may your visions be illuminated.

0. Innocence

"The essential self is innocent, and when it tastes its own innocence knows that it lives forever."
- John Updike

Affirmations:

I am unlimited, I am open, I am a free spirit, I am true to my heart.

Key Words:

Innocence, new path, leap of faith, purity, unlimited potential, free spirit, new phase, trusting flow, feeling protected and loved, being true to self, trusting heart's desire, staying open, recapturing innocence, simplicity, birth, foolish, lack of reasonability, naivety, reckless.

Description:

An infant nestled in a bed of cosmic daisies innocently embarks on a new journey of consciousness and life. During this journey, the infant is protected and guided by twelve hands of the divine while resting in a meditative state of trust. The infant intuitively takes a leap of faith that they will have all that is needed for the journey ahead by firmly holding in its hand belief in the support of the Universe.

Guidance:

I am Innocence. I represent the energy of pureness and potential. I am the vivid dreamer taking a leap of faith into the unknown. Along my path I trust I am divinely guided and protected as I learn and grow from all experiences of life. I am the unfolding flower of consciousness expanding with new beginnings, purity, and faith. I come to you to evoke your own inner being that is pure. I remind you that you are fully supported along your path. Keep in touch with your core innocence and faith. This connection supports your heart and dreams as you take a blind leap into the unknown. Take this opportunity to start a new adventure and dare to be a free spirit; the time is now to be true to your heart and soul by being authentically yourself.

Astrological Planet:

Uranus: *The Rebel Liberator (Rules Aquarius):* Sudden change, seeking freedom in the unknown, breakthroughs, rebirth, genius, inventor, rebel, originality, individuality, sudden change, the awakener**,** unpredictable, shocking, out of the blue, crisis.

Astrological Sign:

Pisces (Water): *The Mystical Visionary:* The soul, third eye, visions, spirituality, dreams, imagination, feelings, impressions, vulnerability, compassion, water, ocean, visionary artist, intuitive, mystic, oracle, psychic, poet, musician, dreamer, spacey, evasive, escapist, vague, abused, deceptive, depressed, foggy, illusory, delusional, passive, confused.

Numerological Vibration: 0

0. Zero: The source of all numbers, increases value of other numbers, male and female, alpha & omega, everything and nothing, potential and choice.

Symbolism:

Infant: Innocence, birth, rebirth, beginnings, protection, divine guidance, growth expansions and the unknown.

Closed Eyes: Peaceful, trusting, innocence, dreams, and the unknown.

Daisies: Innocence, purity, new beginnings, true love, child birth, motherhood.

Open Eye in Left Hand with Spiral Tip: The cosmic force of source, fertility, feminine energy and the womb. A clear channel into a new dimension, pure potential along the physical journey of life. The eye represents the newborns empathic nature which is necessary for him to survive in his new world, trusting his physical vessel has everything it needs within him to support the journey ahead. The spiral is the center of self-expansion to the infinite end of the journey of our souls. The infant's hand also symbolizes human action as well as receiving spirit though the physical vessel.

Twelve Hands: The twelve hands of the divine. The creative source, spirit, guides, and loving consciousness. The circle in the palms flowing with energy represent notions of totality, wholeness, perfection, the infinite, eternity, all cyclical movement, and protection. Twelve symbolizes creative self-expression, cycles of experience though reincarnation.

1. The Creator

"There is vitality, a life force, energy, a quickening that is translated through you into action, and because there is only one of you in all time, this expression is unique." - Martha Graham

Affirmations:

I create, I manifest, I empower, I energize, I will.

Key Words:

Realization, skill, confidence, communication, beginnings, activity, intention, vitality, creating miracles, magic, focused will, emotional intelligence, self-empowerment, what is above is below, creativity, adventure, energy, manifestation, projects, potential, divine masculine, victim mentality, lack of empowerment, unfocused, self-doubt, lack of energy, unaccountability,

Description:

A double-faced unified being representing multidimensional energy peeks through his finger-scope with focused heart, mind, emotions and intention. The Creator manifests physical forms onto the Earth Dimension and no matter which way you turn him, he remains focused with all his energy on his creations. Successfully affirming his spiritual sovereignty, The Creator valiantly embodies, "That which is above in the universe is also below on earth."

Guidance:

I am The Creator. I represent the energy of creation and empowerment. I communicate with universal energy to create and manifest desire into existence. I am the whole-hearted magician creating magic and miracles utilizing Air-Intellect, Fire-Spirit, Earth-Physical, and Water-Emotions. I am the artist of focused intention, will, and potential realized. I represent the bridge between what is above and below. I am the unified power of mind, body, heart, and soul.

I come to remind you of your ability to create your life as you wish. To evoke a new paradigm of creativity, magic, and personal empowerment and to trust in your inner creator. You can manifest your desires. Focus and take this opportunity to tap into your full potential, don't hold back. You have the power to truly create magic. Remember, you are a powerful creator, a spark of all that is.

Go forth with courage and passion in your mind, heart, and soul. Be in love with you, seek a new adventure. It is a choice to believe in oneself for no one else can do it for you. You must do so to maintain inspired momentum and manifestation. To be self-accountable is to be responsible for your life in focused thought, emotion, and action. This is the power of unified consciousness. This is true leadership.

Astrological Planets:

Mercury: *The Messenger of the Spirit (Rules Gemini & Virgo):* Distribution, analyzing, comparing, dualistic, symbolism, communication, categorizing, assimilating, interpretation, short trips, perception, labels, definition, curiosity, experimentation, creativity, language, objective, organized, adaptable, versatile, spontaneous, energetic, youthful, abstract, reflecting, lives in the head, linear thinking, emotionally detached, flaky, unpredictable, unreliable, unfocused, scattered, distracted.

Jupiter: *The Teacher of Expansion and Luck (Rules Sagittarius):* Faith, hope, spiritual and intellectual exploration, higher learning, abstract thinking, religion, philosophy, moral and ethical values, expansion, opportunist, snobbish, egotistical, condescending, cruel, and off-putting.

Astrological Sign:

Aries (Fire): *The Warrior of Power:* Illuminating, consciousness, expressing, energy, activating, essence, vitality, identity, creating, initiating, headstrong, aggressive, risk-taking, rash, impulsive, competitive, egotistical, dominating, pushy, selfish, conflictive.

Numerological Vibration: 1

1. One: Beginnings, independence, creation, foundation of everything, natural born leader, pioneering spirit, uniqueness, motivational, full of energy, vitality, leadership, follower, unmotivated, codependent, apathetic, uninterested, lazy.

Symbolism:

Two Headed Figure: Whichever way you turn The Creator he suggests what is created above is equally created below. The double faces are symbolic of manifesting the universal energy as a unified consciousness of mental, emotional and spiritual intelligence.

Also, indicative of the four elements that The Creator carries in his physical body, air and fire represent mental intelligence and spiritual discernment of his divine masculine energy. Water and earth represent emotional intelligence which is connected to the Feminine intuitive energies and archetype.

Hand Cupping Eye (Finger-Scope): Represents focused energy. the physical, mental and spirit are a unified gateway of creation. Also relates to having a vision of your future and what you desire to create and having focused intention to bring it into your reality, the hand is symbolic of human physical action power and strength, as well as emotional, nurturing and receiving (giving and taking).

The Flower of Life: This pattern of sacred geometry represents that everything is made from The Creator's thoughts and emotions. The Flower of Life contains three dimensions of Metatron's cube which holds all platonic solids, the building blocks of creation itself. Represents creation, success, growth and flowering.

Circles within The Creator's Headdress: Eleven circles in the headdress represent Illumination, a master number in numerology associated with faith, psychics, Intuition, enlightenment, inspirational, idealism special gifts of leadership.

2. The Intuitive

"Vision is the art of seeing what is invisible to others." - Jonathan Swift

Affirmations:

I see, I feel, I hear, I know, I am intuitive, I am receptive, I am psychic, I am guided, I am aware of worlds unseen.

Key Words:

Wisdom, divine feminine, intuition, spirituality, being receptive to influence, emotions, passive, calm, accessing the unconscious, seeking guidance within, open to dreams and imagination, seeing hidden talents and truths, sensing mystery, open to the unknown, seeing that which is hidden, acknowledging the shadow, attunement, psychic ability, denial, doubtful neglect of inner needs, hiding, vague, superficial, fear of making decisions, one sided, reactionary.

Description:

The Intuitive gracefully sits with spiritual sovereignty for she knows that she is birthed from the unlimited creative source. With eyes open from within and without, she is at total peace and unified with her whole being, creating an opening for receiving divine revelations. Her owl companion waits silently to bring additional telepathic messages to and from other dimensions and unseen worlds. Her light radiates from behind her crown of thirteen points, a sacred number for it totals four. Raising her vibration, a doubling of her unified energy of two, yet two points are veiled behind her in obscurity which leaves eleven in sight, a hint to all inquirers to feel and see illumination of balance from within oneself and be open to divine wisdom. She raises her oracular hands mirroring back consciousness, awareness, compassion, peace and service to all that seeks her guidance.

Guidance:

I am The Intuitive. I represent feminine wisdom and intuition. I am the guardian of the unconscious realms. I hold the secrets of the hidden, the obscure, dreams and imagination. I come to guide you to higher learning, awareness, and wisdom, to bring forth a remembrance of the vastness of your intuition and sovereignty. Cradled within you is a kingdom of wealth and knowledge waiting for you to harvest. I ask you to be patient and receptive, and trust that with stillness and balance of oneself you will uncover that which you seek, for in the words of the beloved Sufi mystic Rumi; "That which you seek is seeking you".

Astrological Planets:

Moon: *The Empath of The Subconscious Ocean (Rules Cancer)*: Water, intuition, tides, ebb and flow, feminine, subconscious, reactions, instinct, basic habits, personal needs, co-dependent, inconsistent, easily set off, reactive, overly emotional, depressed, mood swings.

Neptune: *The Channel of Divine Union* (*Rules Pisces)* Spirituality, tranquility, happiness, peace, kindness, mind's eye, intuition, compassion, creation, imagination, magic, miracles, connection, unity, merging, nebulous, mystery, boundless mysticism, letting go, atonement, faith, home, supported, loved, relaxed, illusion, self-deception, escapism, drugs, self-undoing, self-deception, confusion, weakness, self-imprisonment.

Pluto: *The Magician of Empowerment and Transformation (Rules Scorpio)* Death and regeneration, power, control, rebirth, letting go, destruction, profound change, dark night of the soul, surrender, catharsis, emotional release, purification, personal transformation, intense power.

Astrological Signs:

Cancer (Water): *The Empathic Healer:* Energy, tides, ebb and flow, cycles, movement, water, moon, mother intuitive, nurturing, family, home, supportive, provides safety, comfort and foresight, anxious, emotionally attached to the past, touchy, defensive, co-dependent, self-doubting, unstable, high and mighty, afraid, withdrawn, frantic, calculating.

Pisces (Water): *The Mystical Visionary:* The soul, third eye, visions, spirituality, dreams, imagination, feelings, impressions, vulnerability, compassion, water, ocean, visionary artist, intuitive, mystic, oracle, psychic, poet, musician, dreamer, spacey, evasive, escapist, vague, abused, deceptive, depressed, foggy, illusory, delusional, passive, confused.

Numerological Vibration: 2

2. Two: Unity, balance, polarity, diplomatic, service, compassion, nurturing, marriage, co-operation, adaptability, mirroring, relationships, unstable, unbalanced, disturbed, unhinged, one-sided, codependent, coldness.

Symbolism:

The Flower of Life: This pattern of sacred geometry represents that everything is made from The Creator's thoughts and emotions. The Flower of Life contains three dimensions of Metatron's cube which holds all platonic solids, the building blocks of creation itself. Represents creation, success, growth and flowering.

Two Hands Raised: The raised hands symbolize non-threatening peaceful energy and wisdom. Right and left represent action and passive unified. The eyes in the palms are symbolic of inner as well as outer sight, intuition, psychic, empathy, and allowing access and development to clairvoyance, clairsentience, clairaudience and clairvoyance.

Owl: Messenger, wisdom, foresight, keeper of sacred knowledge, living library.

Third Eye: The inner eye provides perception beyond ordinary sight and access to universal knowledge, also associated with the brow chakra.

Blank Eyes: Represents clarity of sight, the mystic, psychic, seer, guardian of realms, empath, intuitive, and medium.

3. The Nurturer

"Everything has beauty, but not everyone sees it". - Confucius

Affirmations:

I nourish, I receive, I give, I am fertile, I bare fruits.

Key Words:

Nourishing life, fertility, motherhood, beauty, gratitude, reception, receiving, tenderness, working with children, welcoming abundance, enjoying the lavish, rewards, luxury, having more than enough, giving, pleasure, appreciating the physical, physical outlet, giving birth, womb, relating to plants and animals, connected to earth, earth mother, harmonious home, neglecting self needs, too much focus on taking care of others, people pleasing, vain, lack of self-love.

Description:

The Nurturer is held in the hands of the divine creative source, providing her with love, beauty, abundance, fertility, creativity, and nourishment. The Nurturer expresses the earthly divine through her potent womb which represents reception, conception and birth.

Guidance:

I am The Nurturer. I represent the life-giving Mother, which encompasses all that is pleasurable, feminine, beautiful and nurturing. I am the fertile womb that receives, conceives and delivers creative life. I represent the hands of love that give and receive the beauty and loving sustenance of care and attention. I am the earthly feminine energy which enjoys receiving bountiful goodness, enchanted with abundance through all my physical senses. I offer you a fertile harvest, gifted with beauty, happiness, pleasure and harmony. All you need to do is be open to receiving these rewards and evoke your own nourishing earth mother. Relax, enjoy and receive all the abundance, love and care of nurturing yourself as well as receiving it from others.

Astrological Planets:

Earth: *The Mother of Nourishment and Growth*: Creative, beautiful, patient, hardworking, practical, grounded, abundant, form, physical, variety, focused, supportive, structure, the four elements - fire, water, air, and earth, stability, protection, harvest, ungrounded, stubborn, unstable, lack, impatient, unfocused, apathetic, destructive, lazy.

Venus: *The Goddess of Love and Beauty (Rules Taurus & Libra):* Confidence, love, beauty, pleasure, sociable, refined, stylish, accommodating, kind, sensual, luxurious, polished, artistic, creative, patron of the arts, overconfident, unfriendly, discontentment, apathetic, bitter, jealous, trite, uninspired, imitative, unoriginal, people pleaser.

Jupiter: *The Teacher of Expansion and Luck (Rules Sagittarius):* Faith, hope, spiritual and intellectual exploration, higher learning, abstract thinking, religion, philosophy, moral and ethical values, expansion, opportunist, snobbish, egotistical, condescending, cruel, and off-putting.

Astrological Signs:

Taurus (Earth): *The Abundant Receiver:* Sustaining, solid, reliable, form, beauty, fruits, stability, reliable, nature, life, structures, sensual, resourceful, dedicated, loyal, strong, predictable, routine, dependable, bullheaded, stubborn, resistant, blocked, unreliable, possessive, idle, dawdling, penny-pinching, defiant, guarded, self-indulgent, rigid, calculating, overprotective.

Cancer (Water): *The Empathic Healer:* Energy, tides, ebb and flow, cycles, movement, water, moon, mother intuitive, nurturing, family, home, supportive, provides safety, comfort and foresight, anxious, emotionally attached to the past, touchy, defensive, co-dependent, self-doubting, unstable, high and mighty, afraid, withdrawn, frantic, calculating.

Libra (Air): *The Beautiful Harmonizer:* Justice, equality, harmony, balance, commitment, artist, spokesperson, diplomat, councilor, lover, event host, politician, uncertain, approval-seeking, cynical, unfocused, procrastinator, passive-aggressive, dishonest, conflicting, unproductive, fickle, teasing, pleasure-seeking, unreliable.

Numerological Vibration: 3

3. Three: Creativity, inspiration, self-expression, joy, triad, catalyst, trinity, manifestation, growth, multiplicity, beginning-middle-end, pyramid, triangle.

Symbolism:

Square Rose Pattern within the Circular Halo: Earth and stability (4 points of the square) combined with the 12-petaled rose rising behind The Nurturer represents the layers of life flowering with spirit and love. The rose represents the goddess Venus. This pattern has 4 (*earth*) layers of 12 points (a higher octave of 3) which equal the sum of 48. 4+8 added together equal 12, 1+2 equal 3, a very creative and noble number. The circle represents wholeness, womb, eternity, cycles, cosmic egg, everything and nothing, potential, purity.

Eight Triangle Crown: Above The Nurturer's head there are 8 triangles with 3 points. 8+3 equals 11 (a higher octave of 2), which represents illumination also connected to the equilibrium and The Intuitive archetypes. The 8 is a doubling of the 4 energy that surrounds the earth elements of The Nurturer.

Hands: The hands represent holding, receiving, giving, nurturing, earth, physical body, DNA, receiving spirit though the body, acceptance, womb, divine protection.

Womb of The Nurturer: The womb shape of The Nurturer's robe and headdress symbolizes fertility, reception, conception, Divine Earth mother, life giving, birth, abundance.

4. The Protector

"Confidence... thrives on honesty, on honor, on the sacredness of obligations, on faithful protection and on unselfish performance." - Franklin D. Roosevelt

Affirmations:
I protect, I defend, I support, I stabilize.

Key Words:
Boundaries, protection, defending, security, organization, leadership, strength, rules, providing shape and form, guidelines, fatherhood, action, guidance, authority, structure, solid foundations, rigid, bossy, demanding, tyrant, lack of boundaries, lack of firm foundation.

Description:
The Protector confidently guards his kingdom with arms spread out to protect and assert his boundaries. He smiles knowing that those allowed to pass him are worthy of his protection and guidance. Those he allows to pass work at building solid foundations towards the greater good of his kingdom.

Guidance:
I am The Protector. I represent the energy of protection. I provide security and defense of self and loved ones. I am the grounded authority of my realms. I am structure and stability. I provide strategy and organization and I stick to my plan and see it through to the end. I come to you offering guidance, protection and structure. I remind you that you have the ability and right to be the authority of your own life, which brings stability, protection of your ideas, and action to manifest those ideas in the physical world. I offer material gain through grounded strategy and guidance. I stand beside you to help you establish healthy boundaries, structured routine, and discipline to help build the foundation of a successful future. Go forth knowing you are a leader who protects what is important to you and know you are supported upon your journey.

Astrological Planet:
Saturn: *The Titan of Trade, Wealth, Agriculture, Work Ethic, and Time. (Rules Capricorn & Aquarius):* Margins, boundaries, accountability, restriction, structure, successful business, responsibilities, commitments, self-control, personal limits, self-empowerment, leadership, harvest, time management, cold, aloof miserly, strict, obstinate, calculating, unfriendly.

Astrological Signs:

Capricorn (Earth): *The Proficient Leader:* Utilizing, practical, concrete, efficient, patient with restrictions, overcoming obstacles, climbing to the top, natural, leadership, aloof, unpractical, impatient, unorganized controlling, bossy, harsh, tyrannical.

Aries (Fire): *The Warrior of Power*: Illuminating, consciousness, expressing energy, activating essence, vitality, identity, creating, initiating, headstrong, aggressive, risk-taking, rash, impulsive, competitive, egotistical, dominating, pushy, selfish, conflictive.

Numerological Vibration: 4

4. Four: Stable, reliable, disciplined, precise, strong, earth, methodical, dependable, hard-working, extracting, conscientious, devoted, loyal, productive.

Symbolism:

The Protector's Stance: Boundaries, protection, authority, confidence.

Horns: Symbol of strength, sovereignty, honor, dignity, earth, the goat.

Wings: Angelic protection, divine source protects all on earth.

Triangles with Eyes: Represents the elements of air and fire, consciousness.

Rising/Setting Sun: Life force, power, strength, energy, self.

Waxing Moon: Growth, manifestation, attainment. Waxing moon is the movement of the new moon increasing in light towards the full moon

Waning Moon: Letting go, contemplation. Waning moon is the movement of the full moon decreasing in light towards the new moon.

Mountains: Earth, boundaries, structure, adventure, stability, conquering and overcoming obstacles, the journey ahead, grounding self, rough terrain, challenges.

5. The Teacher

"When the student is ready, the teacher will appear." - Buddha

Affirmations:

I learn, I know, I guide, I Instruct.

Key Words:

Knowledge, belief systems, studying and learning, increased understanding, cultural heritage, religious traditions, established groups, committed to a cause, divine guidance, mentors, wisdom, devoting energy to an organization, hierophants, high priest, esoteric principles, tradition, conformity, neediness, extreme doctrines, a need to conform to social expectations, loss of personal authority.

Description:

The Teacher appears with hands held up showing you that the wisdom he has to share comes from within him and he blesses with awareness all of those who seek it. A lit candle rests in stillness upon his head which represents his crown of illumination. The pentagram against his chest signifies his personal truth and unified belief of spirit, fire, water, earth and air.

Guidance:

I am The Teacher. I represent belief systems, knowledge and organized education. I am the ancient established structure and tradition within society's institutions and values. I share knowledge through the pursuit of spiritual education, and council. I am the spiritual mentor, the priest, the councilor and the helpful teacher who interprets sacred knowledge and points you in the right direction. I appear to you to offer knowledge and ancient esoteric teachings. I offer you my skills and advice through personal belief systems, organized institutions and teachings. My service of ritualized learning is that you trust as I help guide you with practical wisdom to help you resolve spiritual challenges in your life.

Astrological Planet:

Jupiter: *The Teacher of Expansion and Luck (Rules Sagittarius):* Faith, hope, spiritual and intellectual exploration, higher learning, abstract thinking, religion, philosophy, moral and ethical values, expansion, opportunist, snobbish, egotistical, condescending, cruel, and off-putting.

Astrological Sign:

Taurus (Earth): *The Abundant Receiver:* Sustaining, solid, reliable, form, beauty, fruits, stability, reliable, nature, life, structures, sensual, resourceful, dedicated, loyal, strong, predictable, routine, dependable, bullheaded, stubborn, resistant, blocked, unreliable, possessive, idle, dawdling, penny-pinching, defiant, guarded, self-indulgent, rigid, calculating, overprotective.

Numerological Vibration: 5

5. Five: Constant motion, change, uncompromising demand for freedom, instant gratification, adventurous, teacher of esoteric wisdom, stagnant, stiff, rigid, closed.

Symbolism:

Burning Candle on Head: Represents the illumination and burning light of the activated crown chakra. The lit candle also represents the light in the darkness, holy illumination, ceremonies, spiritual and religious rituals.

Hands Raised with Eyes in Palms: Spiritual awareness, wisdom and guidance.

Pentagram on Chest: Symbol of earth spirituality and magic, the heart chakra, spirit, fire, air, water and earth, the 5 points of the pentagram hint to the numerology of 5 which is change.

The Flower of Life: This pattern of sacred geometry represents that everything is made from The Creator's thoughts and emotions. The Flower of Life contains three dimensions of Metatron's cube which holds all platonic solids, the building blocks of creation itself. Represents creation, success, growth and flowering.

Dot on Forehead: Represents the third eye awakening to the inner eye and sight. Esoteric perception beyond ordinary sight to see what might be or potential.

Triangle Pattern in The Teacher's Hair: Triangles pointing up are the alchemical symbol of fire which represents spirit. Triangles pointing down are the alchemical symbol of water which represents emotion.

6. Love

"Love is all there is." - Emily Dickinson

Affirmations:
I feel with my heart, I relate, I harmonize, I love.

Key Words:
Divine feminine and divine masculine balanced and equal, love, growth, bonds, intimacy, relating to others, union, marriage, kinship, connections, opening to another, attraction, heart consciousness, lovers, family relationships, choices, yin & yang.

Description:
The Divine Feminine and Divine Masculine stand together as one unified force. Balanced and cooperating creates light, love and wholeness within all hearts.

Guidance:
We are Love. We represent the strongest energy of all, a union based on deep and unconditional love that manifests in all loving relationships that involve intimacy and bonds. The light of love is a peaceful consciousness rising in all hearts that are open and willing to receive and to give unconditionally. We follow our hearts unifying female and male energies cooperating as equal parts of the whole. We also represent variety and choice, for love comes in many forms not just romantic partnerships, but all relationships, including the male and female energy within self of giving (male energy) and receiving (feminine energy).

We come to evoke love in your heart, to remind you that a partnership of your head and your heart is wholeness, a marriage of masculine and feminine energy within yourself as well as relationships with others. Bring love and balance of opposing forces to the forefront of your being. Allow the rising light of empathy and compassion to fill your core and shine from the inside out. This unifying light will help illuminate your journey and lead you to your highest good. With an open heart, be confident you will make the best decisions along your path for love is the greatest power of all. When faced with challenges, ask "What would love do in this situation?

Astrological Planets:

Venus: *The Goddess of Love and Beauty (Rules Taurus & Libra):* Confidence, love, beauty, pleasure, sociable, refined, stylish, accommodating, kind, sensual, luxurious, polished, artistic, creative, patron of the arts, overconfident, unfriendly, discontentment, apathetic, bitter, jealous, trite, uninspired, imitative, unoriginal, people pleaser.

Sun: *The Illuminator of Life (Rules Leo):* Illumination, warmth, vitality, success, happiness, light, honors, personal power, expression, empowerment, intense, burning, and overpowering.

Astrological Signs:

Gemini (Air): *The Messenger of Awareness:* Academic, messenger, youth, reflecting, thought, distributing, intelligent, communication, messenger, the writer, intellect, awareness, self-expression, physical and psychological, malleable, youthful, conversant, swift travel, short trips mobile, spur-of-the-moment, bright, insightful, amusing, adaptable, agile, educated, fickle, flakey, two-faced, scattered, surface value, shallow, unattached, sidetracked, anxious, con-artist, self-centered, impish, flimsy, mean, juvenile, confused, and rambling.

Libra (Air): *The Beautiful Harmonizer:* Justice, equality, harmony, balance, commitment, artist, spokesperson, diplomat, councilor, lover, event host, politician, uncertain, approval-seeking, cynical, unfocused, procrastinator, passive-aggressive, dishonest, conflicting, unproductive, fickle, teasing, pleasure-seeking, unreliable.

Leo (Fire): *The Sovereign Performer:* Sovereignty, rulership, courage, self-expression, self-appreciation, playful, kind, open, welcoming, considerate, warm, reliable, energetic, unkind, callous, unreceptive, arrogant, blocked, insensitive, undependable.

Numerological Vibration: 6

6. Six: Harmonic love, magnetic, understanding, compassionate, balanced, nurturing, family, home, affectionate, loving, dependable, reliable, care taker, provider, serving loved ones, self-righteous, critical, people pleasing, negligent, intrusive, nosy, overprotective, unstable.

Symbolism:

Male & Female: Divine Masculine and Feminine energy, polarity, yin yang.

Rose Patterns in Chests of the Divine Archetypes and in Background: Balance, promise, hope, sacrifice, passion, vitality, feeling alive, honor, faith, sensuality, timelessness.

Heart Full of the Rising Sun over the Ocean: The heart represents love and the seat of emotions, the marriage of physical and spiritual awareness. The rising sun represents spirit, fire, passion, love, consciousness, light. This illuminates the marriage of emotions that are, renewal, reflection, purification, intuition, motion, and the subconscious of the ocean.

Divine Masculine Pointing at His Heart: This world is ready to balance the earthly divine masculine. It is time for a shift in the hearts of all of those who have dominant masculine energy to find stillness, peace, true self love, and to learn to balance out male assertiveness with the nurturing reception of the divine feminine.

7. The Master

"Only one who devotes himself to a cause with his whole strength and soul can be a true master. For this reason, mastery demands all of a person." - Albert Einstein

Affirmations:

I master, I focus, I succeed.

Key Words:

Letting nothing distract you, victory, success, focused intent, confidence, faith in accomplishments, self-interests, self-mastery, discipline, balanced ego, will power, determination, movement, travel, distracted, conflict, giving away power, self-defeat.

Description:

The Master stands with arms held high harnessing her energy to stabilize and balance the opposing desires and direction of the fish. The Master commands the slippery sea life to remain entranced with her unified consciousness as she maintains focus to triumph over all obstacles on her path including mastering herself.

Guidance:

I am The Master. I represent will, power, and mastery of opposing forces. I am determination and assertiveness. I am the healthy ego which is strong and self-assured. I know who I am, what I am, and what I want. I succeed in achieving my desires through self-control and determination. I use my will power to bring together opposing forces in self and bring forth everything I need for my journey. With enthusiasm I will reach my destination as my physical vessel is my chariot.

I evoke the remembrance of your own inner master and help you see that you indeed have all the resources you need to master one's self. This helps you maintain balance to succeed in life. Mastery comes with focused intent, action and emotions. Let nothing distract you from achieving what you want, you have the power to claim victory and success.

Astrological Planets:

Sun: *The Illuminator of Life (Rules Leo):* Illumination, warmth, vitality, success, happiness, light, honors, personal power, expression, empowerment, intense, burning, and overpowering.

Moon: *The Empath of The Subconscious Ocean (Rules Cancer)*: Water, intuition, tides, ebb and flow, feminine, subconscious, reactions, instinct, basic habits, personal needs, co-dependent, inconsistent, easily set off, reactive, overly emotional, depressed, mood swings.

Mars: *The Valiant Warrior (Rules Aries & Scorpio):* Active, courage, strength, building, force, energy, leadership, pushing forward, warrior, aggressive, reactive, competitive, combative, conflict, controlling, violence.

Jupiter: *The Teacher of Expansion and Luck (Rules Sagittarius):* Faith, hope, spiritual and intellectual exploration, higher learning, abstract thinking, religion, philosophy, moral and ethical values, expansion, opportunist, snobbish, egotistical, condescending, cruel, and off-putting.

Astrological Signs:

Cancer (Water): *The Empathic Healer:* Energy, tides, ebb and flow, cycles, movement, water, moon, mother intuitive, nurturing, family, home, supportive, provides safety, comfort and foresight, anxious, emotionally attached to the past, touchy, defensive, co-dependent, self-doubting, unstable, high and mighty, afraid, withdrawn, frantic, calculating.

Pisces (Water): *The Mystical Visionary:* The soul, third eye, visions, spirituality, dreams, imagination, feelings, impressions, vulnerability, compassion, water, ocean, visionary artist, intuitive, mystic, oracle, psychic, poet, musician, dreamer, spacey, evasive, escapist, vague, abused, deceptive, depressed, foggy, illusory, delusional, passive, confused.

Leo (Fire): *The Sovereign Performer:* Sovereignty, rulership, courage, self-expression, self-appreciation, playful, kind, open, welcoming, considerate, warm, reliable, energetic, unkind, callous, unreceptive, arrogant, blocked, insensitive, undependable.

Numerological Vibration: 7

7. Seven: Sees the underlying meaning and truth of realities, philosopher, the sage, the seeker of truth, the intellectual, healer, spiritual, psychic, hidden illusions, faith, introspection, spiritual awaking, inner-knowing, the esoteric, negative, rigidity, gloominess, doubtful.

Symbolism:

The Master Balancing/Juggling Opposing Fish: Represents focused willpower to balance opposites within oneself (thought and emotions, air and water) as one powerful unified force. Mastery of feelings, thought, motives, health, and deeper awareness of self-responsibility and power.

The Master's Body: A vessel and vehicle of movement.

The Light Rays behind The Master: Healthy balanced ego/personality/self.

Mountains: Earth, boundaries, structure, adventure, stability, conquering and overcoming obstacles, the journey ahead, grounding self, rough terrain, challenges.

Square Patterns on the Ground and within the Circular Headdress: Stable patterns of thoughts and emotions accomplished by being grounded in oneself (bare feet).

8. Strength

"You have power over your mind - not outside events. Realize this, and you will find strength." - Marcus Aurelius

Affirmations:
I stand my ground, I am courageous, I overcome, I fortify.

Key Words:
Patience, courage, risk, confidence, tempting force, strength of love, compassion, inner strength, overcoming obstacles, instinct, control, confidence, integrity, ego, empowerment, taming the beast.

Description:
The independent lion shows great strength through being present with his environment and calming his animalistic instincts. The quiet king is confident in himself proudly bearing the eight-pointed crown of trust, harmony and strength. The baroque patterns and large eight encompass the lion's mane which shows evidence of earned rewards and badges of honor for his resilient spirit, courageous heart, and faith in the unseen forces.

Guidance:
I am Strength. I represent patience, trust, and courage. I have a resilient character. When faced with challenges, I have the courage to overcome any obstacles of fear. I receive strength from my higher self to tame the lower thoughts, emotions, and behaviors of the reactionary self who is fearful, controlling, destructive, and violent. With an unquenchable will and the energy of the divine guiding me, I have tamed my mind, my emotions, and opened my heart to self-empowerment, strength, and love. I come to you looking to see if your inner lion has awoken to the courage of your heart and soul to tame the animalistic emotions, thoughts, and behaviors that can lead to an unbalanced state of being. This unbalance tends to feed the wounded ego in unhealthy ways. Untamed intellect and emotions are mastered through drawing upon your inner strength and developing patience, resolve, and compassion as you keep going despite setbacks. Be patient, be still, be faithful and be strong.

Astrological Planets:

Sun: *The Illuminator of Life (Rules Leo):* Illumination, warmth, vitality, success, happiness, light, honors, personal power, expression, empowerment, intense, burning, and overpowering.

Mars: *The Valiant Warrior (Rules Aries & Scorpio):* Active, courage, strength, building, force, energy, leadership, pushing forward, warrior, aggressive, reactive, competitive, combative, conflict, controlling, violence.

Astrological Sign:

Leo (Fire): *The Sovereign Performer:* Sovereignty, rulership, courage, self-expression, self-appreciation, playful, kind, open, welcoming, considerate, warm, reliable, energetic, unkind, callous, unreceptive, arrogant, blocked, insensitive, undependable.

Numerological Vibration: **8**

8. Eight: Abundance, material attainment, dependable, efficient, accomplishment, ambition, building useful things for the world, successful management, flourishing, reality, practical, courage, material success, problem solving, organization, impractical, stubborn, lacking ambition, unorganized.

Symbolism:

Lion: Represents taming animal instincts of survival, wild thoughts, and emotions. The calmness of the Lion represents recognizing the strength of mastering self and forgiving weaknesses.

The Star Crown: The strength of trust and making peace in the present moment. Also relates to the 17th archetype The Star. The eight (8) points of the star represent wisdom, patience, personal power and faith.

Baroque Patterns: Comprehensive advancement, badges of honor, rewards.

The Number Eight (8) connected to the Crown's Star: Represents the quality of being in oneself maintaining endurance and stability when confronted with challenges.

9.

The Seeker

"We carry within us the wonders we seek without us." – Thomas Browne

Affirmations:

I seek, I meditate, I discover, I retreat, I understand, I know my truth.

Key Words:

Meditation, light working, withdrawal, inner wisdom, self-discovery, introspective, going inward, looking for answers, seeking greater understanding, awareness and truth, spiritual quest, mentoring, leading by example, wise council, stillness, removing distractions, solitude, peace, closed off, isolated, inaccessible, unhappy, alone, bitter, outlandish, lives on the fringes, un-relatable, self-righteous, narcissistic, small bubble.

Description:

Pensively The Seeker sits alone balanced between the worlds of light and dark. This surreal crossroads of awareness nurtures learning from both the light of the known conscious state of being and the mysterious domain of the unconscious. The shining sun spreads warmth as it rises and sets as it illuminates the juncture of the rotating moons, whose waxing and waning is a dance that embodies the energy of the crescent of giving and receiving.

The Seeker is opulently shrouded in a transformative cloak. He is blessed with the light of the divine through his thirty-six-pointed star illuminating the majestic cocoon and path which brings protection while journeying though both the outer and inner worlds of the universe. Self-initiated seclusion helps focus The Seeker as he centers and proceeds inward to the undiscovered worlds within, understanding himself as a spiritual consciousness experiencing itself as a physical manifestation.

Guidance:

I am The Seeker, I represent withdrawing from the world to seek answers within. I remove myself from distractions of the outer world to focus on exploring my inner world of hearing, feeling and seeing the wisdom and love from spirit. I seek a deeper reality, soul searching for personal spiritual truth and development. I am guided by my inner light of divine inspiration which illuminates the fertile darkness of the unknown. I am the councilor, the guide and the source of eternal light through the darkness.

I come to you to look out for and gently guide you while you are looking within yourself for god, the creative source, and answers you seek. I remind you to search for deeper truth in your life and honor self-examination and reflection. Let go of outside distractions while you maintain solitude away from society, do not let anything discourage you from embarking upon this journey. As you seek so shall you find, you are your own mentor, guide, and master. So, go forth and claim your new-found perspective and truth, the doors of consciousness are before you waiting to be claimed, opened, and explored.

Astrological Planets:

Neptune: *The Channel of Divine Union* (*Rules Pisces)* Spirituality, tranquility, happiness, peace, kindness, mind's eye, intuition, compassion, creation, imagination, magic, miracles, connection, unity, merging, nebulous, mystery, boundless mysticism, letting go, atonement, faith, home, supported, loved, relaxed, illusion, self-deception, escapism, drugs, self-undoing, self-deception, confusion, weakness, self-imprisonment.

Uranus: *The Rebel Liberator (Rules Aquarius):* Sudden change, seeking freedom in the unknown, breakthroughs, rebirth, genius, inventor, rebel, originality, individuality, sudden change, the awakener**,** unpredictable, shocking, out of the blue, crisis.

Pluto: *The Magician of Empowerment and Transformation (Rules Scorpio)* Death and regeneration, power, control, rebirth, letting go, destruction, profound change, dark night of the soul, surrender, catharsis, emotional release, purification, personal transformation, intense power.

Astrological Signs:

Virgo (Earth): *The Methodical Organizer:* Reflecting, demonstrating, analytical, modest, intelligent, selective, methodical, discerning, discriminating devoted, strong, wholesome, service-oriented, sensible, reserved, astute, resourceful, diligent, critical, perfectionist, self-effacing, capricious, picky, tense, self-conscious, worrier, and the willing victim.

Pisces (Water): *The Mystical Visionary:* The soul, third eye, visions, spirituality, dreams, imagination, feelings, impressions, vulnerability, compassion, water, ocean, visionary artist, intuitive, mystic, oracle, psychic, poet, musician, dreamer, spacey, evasive, escapist, vague, abused, deceptive, depressed, foggy, illusory, delusional, passive, confused.

Sagittarius (Fire): *The Free-Spirited Adventurer*: Ambitious, positive, optimist, wit, sincere, clear-cut, spur-of-the-moment, enthusiastic, thoughtful, philosophical, candid, open-minded, edification, publishing, tactless, domineering, arrogant, fanatical, dogmatic, patronizing, unbalanced ego, rambling, careless, irresponsible, restless, aloof, emotionally detached.

Scorpio (Water): *The Powerful Mysterious Psychic*: Powerful, intense, passionate, inquisitive, magnetic, deep, fierce, mysterious, psychic, esoteric, cryptic, sexy, seductive, faithful, secretive, mesmerizing, envious, magical, observant, obsessive, dark, calculating, compulsive, complicated, jealous, irritable.

Cancer (Water): *The Empathic Healer:* Energy, tides, ebb and flow, cycles, movement, water, moon, mother intuitive, nurturing, family, home, supportive, provides safety, comfort and foresight, anxious, emotionally attached to the past, touchy, defensive, co-dependent, self-doubting, unstable, high and mighty, afraid, withdrawn, frantic, calculating.

Numerological Vibration: 9

9. Nine: Universal energies, inner wisdom, responsibility, service to humanity, compassion, selflessness, protective energy, love of nature and earth, light working, service, benevolent, selfless, advanced souls, stressed, uptight, trying to solve everyone's problems, willing victim, overbearing, dogmatic, self-righteous.

Symbolism:

The Seeker: Vessel of the inner worlds, light working, leading by example, putting light in dark places.

Turban and Cloak: All is shrouded but for the eyes of the seeker representing focused vision, quest of consciousness, withdrawal, and going inward.

Blank/White Eyes: Altered states of consciousness, multidimensional facets of consciousness and life, trance states, channeling and psychic mediumship.

Thirty-Six (36) Pointed Star within the Circle: Represents divine illumination of trust and faith along your path and during your quests. Numerological value of three (3) sets of twelve (12) points of the star equal thirty-six (36). Three (3) and six (6) added together come to a nine (9) mirroring and representing the nine (9) position of the seeker's numerological archetypal vibration. The circle indicates wholeness. The position of the star represents the pineal gland, the portal of self and the creative source of God and the Universe.

The Sun and Moon: Light and dark aspects of the journey ahead moving through understanding states of being and awareness as physical manifestation. Uniting and balancing the ebb and flow of self-awareness through intellect and emotions through the unconscious self.

Mountains: Earth, boundaries, structure, adventure, stability, conquering and overcoming obstacles, the journey ahead, grounding self, rough terrain, challenges.

10. The Circle of Prosperity

"Abundance is not something we acquire. It is something we tune into." - Wayne Dyer

Affirmations:

I expand, I change, I shift, I succeed, I receive, I give.

Key Words:

Awareness of how everything is connected, expansive energy, renewal, growth, cycles, change, turning point, altering and changing vibration, changes in abundance, new development, personal vision, balance, expansion of awareness and trust, discovering your life path, success.

Description:

A peaceful woman sits in a yoga position as she meditates on her prosperity, expansion and success along her life path. She balances her vibrations of male and female energy which mirror the sun and the moon polarity of mental intellect and the feelings and reception of emotional intelligence. This unified partnership creates stability and creative power while the world around her shifts and sheds its skin. Prosperity and seeds of creation are given out through her thoughts and pulled back and received by her emotions. In this, she gives as she takes and is successfully mastering the revolution of the infinite circle of prosperity.

Guidance:

I am The Circle of Prosperity. I represent cycles, expansion, and successful renewal. I am creating my life though expanding my consciousness of mind, body, and soul. I give thanks to the ever-expanding circle of prosperity for it supports me as I allow growth through the practice of equally giving and receiving. I develop new visions and opportunities. I bring discovery and represent the ultimate turning point of wealth and creativity.

I maintain a balance of the perception of my emotional state of being with my mental intentions and focus. This balance is a powerful focal point of energy which manifests fruits of abundance and prosperity. These gifts are accelerated with a consciousness of heart and mind that lives in the love of gratitude for all the magical gifts given and received from the great creative source and our sovereign mother Gaia.

I come to you to present the energy and momentum of universal expansion that is within your mercurial circle of life. I help you see your expansion through synchronicities, omens and co–creation. Recognize the path flowering before you, this is the indication you are consciously creating your life and the fruits around you. This turning point is to help you trust your sense of purpose and succeed as you move through life's cycles of prosperity with ease and grace through the challenges of the journey. Understand you create your own reality. Your state of being affects which opportunities or situations come to you in your life, none are by mistake. If you are struggling with a difficult situation or lack of growth, I come to remind you that you will find the answer when you view it from a larger perspective of a unified heart and mind.

Astrological Planets:

Jupiter: *The Teacher of Expansion and Luck (Rules Sagittarius):* Faith, hope, spiritual and intellectual exploration, higher learning, abstract thinking, religion, philosophy, moral and ethical values, expansion, opportunist, snobbish, egotistical, condescending, cruel, and off-putting.

Sun: *The Illuminator of Life (Rules Leo):* Illumination, warmth, vitality, success, happiness, light, honors, personal power, expression, empowerment, intense, burning, and overpowering.

Moon: *The Empath of The Subconscious Ocean (Rules Cancer)*: Water, intuition, tides, ebb and flow, feminine, subconscious, reactions, instinct, basic habits, personal needs, co-dependent, inconsistent, easily set off, reactive, overly emotional, depressed, mood swings.

Earth: *The Mother of Nourishment and Growth*: Creative, beautiful, patient, hardworking, practical, grounded, abundant, form, physical, variety, focused, supportive, structure, the four elements - fire, water, air, and earth, stability, protection, harvest, ungrounded, stubborn, unstable, lack, impatient, unfocused, apathetic, destructive, lazy.

Astrological Sign:

Sagittarius (Fire): *The Free-Spirited Adventurer*: Ambitious, positive, optimist, wit, sincere, clear-cut, spur-of-the-moment, enthusiastic, thoughtful, philosophical, candid, open-minded, edification, publishing, tactless, domineering, arrogant, fanatical, dogmatic, patronizing, unbalanced ego, rambling, careless, irresponsible, restless, aloof, emotionally detached.

Taurus (Earth): *The Abundant Receiver:* Sustaining, solid, reliable, form, beauty, fruits, stability, reliable, nature, life, structures, sensual, resourceful, dedicated, loyal, strong, predictable, routine, dependable, bullheaded, stubborn, resistant, blocked, unreliable, possessive, idle, dawdling, penny-pinching, defiant, guarded, self-indulgent, rigid, calculating, overprotective.

Numerological Vibration: 10

0. Zero: The source of all numbers, increases value of other numbers, male and female, alpha & omega, everything and nothing, potential and choice.

(The Total Numerological Vibration is 1)

1. One: Beginnings, independence, creation, foundation of everything, natural born leader, pioneering spirit, uniqueness, motivational, full of energy, vitality, leadership, follower, unmotivated, codependent, apathetic, uninterested, lazy.

Symbolism:

Meditating Woman: Being receptive, expansive consciousness, peaceful journeys and dreams, having faith and focused momentum, balance.

The Flower of Life: This pattern of sacred geometry represents that everything is made from The Creator's thoughts and emotions. The Flower of Life contains three dimensions of Metatron's cube which holds all platonic solids, the building blocks of creation itself. Represents creation, success, growth and flowering.

The Ouroboros Snake- Cycles, shifts, patterns, ebb and flow, renewal, wholeness.

The Sun and Moon: Light and dark aspects of the journey ahead moving through understanding states of being and awareness as physical manifestation. Uniting and balancing the ebb and flow of self-awareness through intellect and emotions through the unconscious self.

Mountains: Earth, boundaries, structure, adventure, stability, conquering and overcoming obstacles, the journey ahead, grounding self, rough terrain, challenges.

11. Equilibrium

"Before God we are all equally wise - and equally foolish." - Albert Einstein

Affirmations:

I balance, I synchronize, I validate.

Key Words:

Balance, equality, equilibrium, fairness, justice, accountability, cause and effect, weighing all sides, choosing with awareness and impartiality.

Description:

Equilibrium stands candidly upholding her sacred oath of fairness. Emanating from her is justice and balance of opposing forces, and through this unbiased energy stability is attained. She holds space for balance wherever she goes and for whomever calls upon her. Her decision is unbiased, for both sides are equal in her care.

Guidance:

I am Equilibrium. I represent the energy force of balance, fairness and equality. I weigh all sides with impartiality and I am aware of justice through being accountable of cause and effect. I come to you providing balance to remind you of divine harmony, fairness, and balance of personal discernment in all areas your life, light and dark, and the conscious and unconscious parts of one's self.

I help you access the level playing field of self-assessment regarding choices and behaviors of self and others, especially regarding relationships. I help bring back balance to extreme reactive situations. Balance is to choose with neutral awareness, and I encourage you to be accountable for your actions thoughts and emotions. Be honest and fair while making decisions for self and regarding others.

Astrological Planets:

Venus: *The Goddess of Love and Beauty (Rules Taurus & Libra):* Confidence, love, beauty, pleasure, sociable, refined, stylish, accommodating, kind, sensual, luxurious, polished, artistic, creative, patron of the arts, overconfident, unfriendly, discontentment, apathetic, bitter, jealous, trite, uninspired, imitative, unoriginal, people pleaser.

Mercury: *The Messenger of the Spirit (Rules Gemini & Virgo):* Distribution, analyzing, comparing, dualistic, symbolism, communication, categorizing, assimilating, interpretation, short trips, perception, labels, definition, curiosity, experimentation, creativity, language, objective, organized, adaptable, versatile, spontaneous, energetic, youthful, abstract, reflecting, lives in the head, linear thinking, emotionally detached, flaky, unpredictable, unreliable, unfocused, scattered, distracted.

Saturn: *The Titan of Trade, Wealth, Agriculture, Work Ethic, and Time. (Rules Capricorn & Aquarius):* Margins, boundaries, accountability, restriction, structure, successful business, responsibilities, commitments, self-control, personal limits, self-empowerment, leadership, harvest, time management, cold, aloof miserly, strict, obstinate, calculating, unfriendly.

Jupiter: *The Teacher of Expansion and Luck (Rules Sagittarius):* Faith, hope, spiritual and intellectual exploration, higher learning, abstract thinking, religion, philosophy, moral and ethical values, expansion, opportunist, snobbish, egotistical, condescending, cruel, and off-putting.

Astrological Signs:

Libra (Air): *The Beautiful Harmonizer:* Justice, equality, harmony, balance, commitment, artist, spokesperson, diplomat, councilor, lover, event host, politician, uncertain, approval-seeking, cynical, unfocused, procrastinator, passive-aggressive, dishonest, conflicting, unproductive, fickle, teasing, pleasure-seeking, unreliable.

Gemini (Air): *The Messenger of Awareness*: Academic, messenger, youth, reflecting, thought, distributing, intelligent, communication, messenger, the writer, intellect, awareness, self-expression, physical and psychological, malleable, youthful, conversant, swift travel, short trips mobile, spur-of-the-moment, bright, insightful, amusing, adaptable, agile, educated, fickle, flakey, two-faced, scattered, surface value, shallow, unattached, sidetracked, anxious, con-artist, self-centered, impish, flimsy, mean, juvenile, confused, and rambling.

Pisces (Water): *The Mystical Visionary:* The soul, third eye, visions, spirituality, dreams, imagination, feelings, impressions, vulnerability, compassion, water, ocean, visionary artist, intuitive, mystic, oracle, psychic, poet, musician, dreamer, spacey, evasive, escapist, vague, abused, deceptive, depressed, foggy, illusory, delusional, passive, confused.

Numerological Vibration: 11

11. Eleven: Illumination, double layer of the Two vibration, master number, light, psychic abilities, mediumship, energy, seer, mystic, magnetic, dreamer, visionary, higher energy, enlightenment, awakening, consciousness, altered states of being, magic, receptive, creative, teaching, ungrounded, overly empathic, psychic sponge, no boundaries, live wire, hurt, raw, confused, willing victim giving power away.

(The Total Numerological Vibration is 2)

2. Two: Unity, balance, polarity, diplomatic, service, compassion, nurturing, marriage, co-operation, adaptability, mirroring, relationships, unstable, unbalanced, disturbed, unhinged, one-sided, codependent, coldness.

Symbolism:

Eyes: Consciousness, awareness, visions, sight, and review.

Hands Up: Impartiality, unbiased and fairness.

Equilibrium and the Opposing Beings: Represent the scales of Justice.

Emanating Light: Illumination, self-accountability.

12. Surrender

"Some of us think holding on makes us strong; but sometimes it is letting go."

- Hermann Hesse

Affirmations:

I surrender, I let go, I detach, I release.

Key Words:

Letting go, emotional release, accepting what is, surrendering to experience, giving up control, change of mind, viewing from a new perspective, suspension of action, being in the moment, sacrifice, time out, detachment.

Description:

An ornate woman willingly practices surrender to achieve self-truth, illumination and enlightenment. Her eyes closed in ecstasy for she is enraptured with the vast inner world of spirit. She lets go of unimportant needs, control and beliefs that were once the focus and aspiration of her unconscious wounded ego. Now in search of a more authentic way of life, this self-sacrifice of letting go of what no longer serves her greatest good and soul mission is sought in faith of obtaining wisdom, insight, and personal expansion.

Guidance:

I am Surrender. I represent the energy and act of letting go and releasing control, old emotions, beliefs, and pursuits that do not bring me happiness, expansion and personal truth. I accept this suspended action and personal sacrifice by viewing life from a new perspective. I surrender to the ecstasy of being in the moment. I receive personal power by letting go of the need to know how, and when things will work out. I move forward by letting go of struggle and control and allow everything to flow as it is, for the unknown is to be trusted with the heart, not feared by the mind.

I come to remind you that letting go and surrendering is not a weakness. It is a great strength to detach and trust in the unfolding events around and within you. When you release the tight grip of control, energy is released within and around you, creating synchronicities and support that are more in line with your new perspective on life goals and desires. So, let go of controlling the situation, surrender to faith in the universe and self.

Astrological Planets:

Neptune: *The Channel of Divine Union (**Rules Pisces**)* Spirituality, tranquility, happiness, peace, kindness, mind's eye, intuition, compassion, creation, imagination, magic, miracles, connection, unity, merging, nebulous, mystery, boundless mysticism, letting go, atonement, faith, home, supported, loved, relaxed, illusion, self-deception, escapism, drugs, self-undoing, self-deception, confusion, weakness, self-imprisonment.

Pluto: *The Magician of Empowerment and Transformation (Rules Scorpio)* Death and regeneration, power, control, rebirth, letting go, destruction, profound change, dark night of the soul, surrender, catharsis, emotional release, purification, personal transformation, intense power.

Uranus: *The Rebel Liberator (Rules Aquarius):* Sudden change, seeking freedom in the unknown, breakthroughs, rebirth, genius, inventor, rebel, originality, individuality, sudden change, the awakener**,** unpredictable, shocking, out of the blue, crisis.

Astrological Sign:

Pisces (Water): *The Mystical Visionary:* The soul, third eye, visions, spirituality, dreams, imagination, feelings, impressions, vulnerability, compassion, water, ocean, visionary artist, intuitive, mystic, oracle, psychic, poet, musician, dreamer, spacey, evasive, escapist, vague, abused, deceptive, depressed, foggy, illusory, delusional, passive, confused.

Numerological Vibration: 12

1. One: Beginnings, independence, creation, foundation of everything, natural born leader, pioneering spirit, uniqueness, motivational, full of energy, vitality, leadership, follower, unmotivated, codependent, apathetic, uninterested, lazy.

2. Two: Unity, balance, polarity, diplomatic, service, compassion, nurturing, marriage, co-operation, adaptability, mirroring, relationships, unstable, unbalanced, disturbed, unhinged, one-sided, codependent, coldness.

(The Total Numerological Vibration is 3)

3. Three: Creativity, inspiration, self-expression, joy, triad, catalyst, trinity, manifestation, growth, multiplicity, beginning-middle-end, pyramid, triangle.

Symbolism:

Woman: Head back, eyes closed, symbolic of surrender letting go, being still in self, emotional, mental, spiritual surrender to something bigger, giving up control, giving up fear.

Circles: Trust in spirit, wholeness, cycles, unity of the mind and the heart, intellect, emotional intelligence.

Flower Pattern: Represents growth through surrender to life.

Star Background Pattern: Faith and trust in the unseen forces that are helping and protecting us, also a nod to the archetype The Star.

13. Death

"Death may be the greatest of all human blessings." - Socrates

Affirmations:
I die, I transform, I change, I transmute I complete.

Key Words:
Putting the past behind you, moving from the known to the unknown, death, metamorphosis, endings, completion, transition, eliminating excess, shedding old perspectives, the inevitable, powerful movement, renewal, change, transformation, mourning, loss, rebirth.

Description:
Death offers new life if you give him your old debris and decay. He represents physical death, but more so an epitome of ending old cycles, situations, and transformation for the better.

Death shows up to take what has been used up and that which is dying within you, an unavoidable contract of new life in exchange of the old, rotting in stagnation. His intense stare announces his seriousness for he will take what is no longer useful and outdated be you ready or not. It can be done the easy way or the hard way, but none the less he will reap all that is rancid and finished. None can overcome death for it is necessary for growth. You can work with him as he offers you a brand-new life or helplessly cling to what is rotting as he seizes it from you. Ending what you once were leads to being birthed anew. Death is not to be feared but to be celebrated.

Guidance:
I am Death. I represent the energy of transmutation, change and rebirth. I am the powerful guardian of the unknown and the known, life and death, endings and beginnings, old and new. I take your past in exchange for your future. I take what is outdated and no longer serving your highest good. I come to you to offer life through death, for only when you release to me what is no longer serving you can you be birthed anew. The endings may be difficult and painful, but you must learn to accept these endings though a period of mourning and amendment before you can move onto a new path. Allow yourself to come to terms with releasing the old and you shall transform into a beautiful butterfly for I offer you life if you give me your chrysalis of decay.

Astrological Planets:

Mars: *The Valiant Warrior (Rules Aries & Scorpio):* Active, courage, strength, building, force, energy, leadership, pushing forward, warrior, aggressive, reactive, competitive, combative, conflict, controlling, violence.

Pluto: *The Magician of Empowerment and Transformation (Rules Scorpio)* Death and regeneration, power, control, rebirth, letting go, destruction, profound change, dark night of the soul, surrender, catharsis, emotional release, purification, personal transformation, intense power.

Saturn: *The Titan of Trade, Wealth, Agriculture, Work Ethic, and Time. (Rules Capricorn & Aquarius):* Margins, boundaries, accountability, restriction, structure, successful business, responsibilities, commitments, self-control, personal limits, self-empowerment, leadership, harvest, time management, cold, aloof miserly, strict, obstinate, calculating, unfriendly.

Uranus: *The Rebel Liberator (Rules Aquarius):* Sudden change, seeking freedom in the unknown, breakthroughs, rebirth, genius, inventor, rebel, originality, individuality, sudden change, the awakener, unpredictable, shocking, out of the blue, crisis.

Astrological Sign:

Scorpio (Water): *The Powerful Mysterious Psychic*: Powerful, intense, passionate, inquisitive, magnetic, deep, fierce, mysterious, psychic, esoteric, cryptic, sexy, seductive, faithful, secretive, mesmerizing, envious, magical, observant, obsessive, dark, calculating, compulsive, complicated, jealous, irritable.

Numerological Vibration: 13

1. One: Beginnings, independence, creation, foundation of everything, natural born leader, pioneering spirit, uniqueness, motivational, full of energy, vitality, leadership, follower, unmotivated, codependent, apathetic, uninterested, lazy.

3. Three: Creativity, inspiration, self-expression, joy, triad, catalyst, trinity, manifestation, growth, multiplicity, beginning-middle-end, pyramid, triangle.

(The Total Numerological Vibration is 4)

4. Four: Stable, reliable, disciplined, precise, strong, earth, methodical, dependable, hard-working, extracting, conscientious, devoted, loyal, productive.

Symbolism:

Death Archetype: Death, change, transformation, guardian of life and death.

Butterflies: The butterflies in the background and inside the robe of death represent outer and inner transformation, movement, growth, freedom, transmutation, earning your wings.

Infant: Innocence, birth, rebirth, beginnings, protection, divine guidance, growth expansions and the unknown.

Chrysalis: The shell of transformation, what is no longer useful, past, decay.

14. Synthesis

"How can we know the dancer from the dance?" - William Butler Yeats

Affirmations:

I synthesize, I moderate, I unite, I harmonize.

Key Words:

A beautiful dance bringing together opposites, combination, balance, temperance, middle ground, moderation, compromise, harmony, synthesis, centered, vigor, energy, vitality, flourishing, secure, wellbeing, hope, rhythm, graceful composure.

Description:

Suspended in the dreamy space of source and creation, a dance has begun. A unity composed of love and respect for each other's uniqueness, the dancers create an expansive new energy. Nothing can separate this synthesis of opposites for the merging has been experienced as one.

Guidance:

We are Synthesis. We represent the energy of harmony, grace, and temperance. We dance and create vitality with balanced rhythm as we express and merge our unique energies together offering something new to one another and the world. Our fluid dance is a graceful composure of wellbeing through freedom to be oneself and cooperation. We move with calm deliberation, bringing comfort though harmony, centering, and self-restraint.

We offer moderation, patience, health, and wellbeing. We bring to you the energy of give and take, solutions, and the ability to manage and resolve problems. We remind you events will be smooth and will bring harmonious relationships, cooperative situations, and synchronicities. Be centered and create synthesis through self-composure and the dance you have with yourself and the infinite creative source.

Astrological Planets:

Mercury: *The Messenger of the Spirit (Rules Gemini & Virgo):* Distribution, analyzing, comparing, dualistic, symbolism, communication, categorizing, assimilating, interpretation, short trips, perception, labels, definition, curiosity, experimentation, creativity, language, objective, organized, adaptable, versatile, spontaneous, energetic, youthful, abstract, reflecting, lives in the head, linear thinking, emotionally detached, flaky, unpredictable, unreliable, unfocused, scattered, distracted.

Venus: *The Goddess of Love and Beauty (Rules Taurus & Libra):* Confidence, love, beauty, pleasure, sociable, refined, stylish, accommodating, kind, sensual, luxurious, polished, artistic, creative, patron of the arts, overconfident, unfriendly, discontentment, apathetic, bitter, jealous, trite, uninspired, imitative, unoriginal, people pleaser.

Neptune: *The Channel of Divine Union* (***Rules Pisces***) Spirituality, tranquility, happiness, peace, kindness, mind's eye, intuition, compassion, creation, imagination, magic, miracles, connection, unity, merging, nebulous, mystery, boundless mysticism, letting go, atonement, faith, home, supported, loved, relaxed, illusion, self-deception, escapism, drugs, self-undoing, self-deception, confusion, weakness, self-imprisonment.

Astrological Signs:

Libra (Air): *The Beautiful Harmonizer:* Justice, equality, harmony, balance, commitment, artist, spokesperson, diplomat, councilor, lover, event host, politician, uncertain, approval-seeking, cynical, unfocused, procrastinator, passive-aggressive, dishonest, conflicting, unproductive, fickle, teasing, pleasure-seeking, unreliable.

Gemini (Air): *The Messenger of Awareness*: Academic, messenger, youth, reflecting, thought, distributing, intelligent, communication, messenger, the writer, intellect, awareness, self-expression, physical and psychological, malleable, youthful, conversant, swift travel, short trips mobile, spur-of-the-moment, bright, insightful, amusing, adaptable, agile, educated, fickle, flakey, two-faced, scattered, surface value, shallow, unattached, sidetracked, anxious, con-artist, self-centered, impish, flimsy, mean, juvenile, confused, and rambling.

Pisces (Water): *The Mystical Visionary:* The soul, third eye, visions, spirituality, dreams, imagination, feelings, impressions, vulnerability, compassion, water, ocean, visionary artist, intuitive, mystic, oracle, psychic, poet, musician, dreamer, spacey, evasive, escapist, vague, abused, deceptive, depressed, foggy, illusory, delusional, passive, confused.

Aquarius (Air): *The Cosmic Intuitive Genius:* Open, progressive, vast, remarkable, intelligent, original, restructuring, sovereign, peculiar, liberal, inventive, drastic, outrageous, erratic, detached, obstinate, scandalous, spacey, weird, troublemaking, mechanized, impulsive, fanatical, unreasonable, mutinous, inflexible.

Numerological Vibration: 14

1. One: Beginnings, independence, creation, foundation of everything, natural born leader, pioneering spirit, uniqueness, motivational, full of energy, vitality, leadership, follower, unmotivated, codependent, apathetic, uninterested, lazy.

4. Four: Stable, reliable, disciplined, precise, strong, earth, methodical, dependable, hard-working, extracting, conscientious, devoted, loyal, productive.

(The Total Numerological Vibration is 5)

5. Five: Constant motion, change, uncompromising demand for freedom, instant gratification, adventurous, teacher of esoteric wisdom, stagnant, stiff, rigid, closed.

Symbolism:

Women Dancing: Creating something new from opposing forces harmony, wellbeing, energy, vitality, grace, creation, synthesis.

Eyes Closed: Wellbeing, enjoyment, merging with source and one another.

Flowing Hair with Flower Petal Patterns: Vitality, health, growth, energy fluidity, beauty, flourishing.

Spirals: Cosmic mind, force, expansion, unlimited.

Bare Breasts: Openness, vulnerability, nourishment, femininity, receiving.

Background Pattern: Water and fire, waves (water) and reptile scales (fire)

15. Fear

"The only thing we have to fear is fear itself." - Franklin D. Roosevelt

Affirmations:

I fear, I doubt, I lack, I restrict, I consume, I expel, I enslave.

Key Words:

Bondage, lack, doubt, obsession, loss, control, addiction, enslavement, vampirism, submitting your power to another, hyper focused on materialism, forgetting the spiritual part of self, choosing to stay in the dark, paralysis, bleak, draining, expecting the worse, lack of faith, negativity, self-defeat, victimization, unbalanced, the shadow self.

Description:

Fear is all consuming. If you agree to dance with this devil, it spews forth lies that attach to one's beliefs like a parasite. The agenda of fear is to enslave those in its grasp, encouraging one to believe negative energy. This vampiric force consists of both male and female polarity that play off each other's disfunction. Fear lures the mind and emotions with the promise of short term material gratification and the illusion of perfection of the ego self. Fear is a teacher that shows us that we have a choice to believe in the lies of oppression or our natural state of being which is love.

Guidance:

We are Fear, we represent the energy of darkness, doubt and negativity. We embody the shadow of lies that convince your consciousness, both in mind and in body to focus upon fear instead of love. We solicit to you that you are only safe if you stay small, miserable, and inauthentic to the real you. We keep you enslaved to a false truth, a false god, blind to the light of your true self. We love that you go into hiding from expressing your true self as we drain you of your vitality and zest for life. We represent the sinking darkness that consumes you. We promote an addiction to lack, lies and illusion. We convince you that you are separate and unworthy of true self-empowerment and self-worth. We peddle fear at every angle sending out vast rockets of soldiers armed with self-effacement, anxiety, and pain. Belief in fear creates a loop system of negative experiences from habitual affirmations of lack, unworthiness, and victimization. Fear paralyzes you and keeps you from growing, but also alerts you to the fact you are so greatly empowered that you can choose abundance or lack, fear or love, so thus you are powerful in any emotional thought or feeling you consistently focus on.

Examine your beliefs about yourself and try to understand are they yours or lies you bought into? Are you seeing yourself as your true self, or disconnected from source and your highest good? Fear is helpful in small doses when we are in threat of physical danger. Fear guides you away from dangerous people or situations, yet dwelling in fear beyond the immediate danger will only bring smallness and lack.

Astrological Planets:

Saturn: *The Titan of Trade, Wealth, Agriculture, Work Ethic, and Time. (Rules Capricorn & Aquarius):* Margins, boundaries, accountability, restriction, structure, successful business, responsibilities, commitments, self-control, personal limits, self-empowerment, leadership, harvest, time management, cold, aloof miserly, strict, obstinate, calculating, unfriendly.

Pluto: *The Magician of Empowerment and Transformation (Rules Scorpio)* Death and regeneration, power, control, rebirth, letting go, destruction, profound change, dark night of the soul, surrender, catharsis, emotional release, purification, personal transformation, intense power.

Astrological Signs:

Scorpio (Water): *The Powerful Mysterious Psychic*: Powerful, intense, passionate, inquisitive, magnetic, deep, fierce, mysterious, psychic, esoteric, cryptic, sexy, seductive, faithful, secretive, mesmerizing, envious, magical, observant, obsessive, dark, calculating, compulsive, complicated, jealous, irritable.

Capricorn (Earth): *The Proficient Leader:* Utilizing, practical, concrete, efficient, patient with restrictions, overcoming obstacles, climbing to the top, natural, leadership, aloof, unpractical, impatient, unorganized controlling, bossy, harsh, tyrannical.

Aries (Fire): *The Warrior of Power:* Illuminating, consciousness, expressing, energy, activating, essence, vitality, identity, creating, initiating, headstrong, aggressive, risk-taking, rash, impulsive, competitive, egotistical, dominating, pushy, selfish, conflictive.

Numerological Vibration: 15

1. One: Beginnings, independence, creation, foundation of everything, natural born leader, pioneering spirit, uniqueness, motivational, full of energy, vitality, leadership, follower, unmotivated, codependent, apathetic, uninterested, lazy.

5. Five: Constant motion, change, uncompromising demand for freedom, instant gratification, adventurous, teacher of esoteric wisdom, stagnant, stiff, rigid, closed.

(The Total Numerological Vibration is 6)

6. Six: Harmonic love, magnetic, understanding, compassionate, balanced, nurturing, family, home, affectionate, loving, dependable, reliable, care taker, provider, serving loved ones, self-righteous, critical, people pleasing, negligent, intrusive, nosy, overprotective, unstable.

Symbolism:

Inverted Pentagram: Unbalance, out of synch with higher self and source, unbalanced emotions, (water), body (earth), thoughts (air), spirit (fire), the Upright Pentagram is about balance and harmony.

Female & Male Archetypes: Yin and Yang, being and doing, giving and receiving polarity.

Female Expelling and Consuming Male: Vampirism, consumption, obsession, drains, life force, expelling, negative energy.

Double Image: Mirroring, shadow.

Background Webbing: Energy, field of consciousness, universal energy, magnetic field, web of life we are all connected to.

16. Upheaval

"The crisis of today is the joke of tomorrow." – H.G. Wells

Affirmations:

I expose, I crumble, I collapse, I struggle, I change, I purify.

Key Words:

Sudden realization of the truth, exposing what has been hidden, seeing though illusions, breaking down barriers of consciousness, collapsing false walls around the heart and soul, upheaval, sudden change, chaos, exploding anger, outbursts, being shocked and surprised, crisis, ego defenses, insecurity, shock, loss struggle.

Description:

Upon unstable ground, a fortress conceals old beliefs, hurts, and false ideals of the personality and ego. As higher consciousness of the soul approaches the walls of the fortress, vampiric alarms expressing shock, anger, and unconsciousness react to the presence of spirit, truth, love, and light. The light illuminates and heals the repressed emotions, memories, suffering and pain hiding within its walls. The screaming alarms have been positioned by the wounded ego to maintain security and control over all circumstances and it becomes the driving force of motivation and behaviors to always protect the wound, yet never attempt to heal it.

Guidance:

I am Upheaval. I represent crisis, defense, and the fortress of the wounded. I scream at any threat that approaches my walls. The brick wall represents the wounded ego, which was built of ambition to keep oneself safe, yet constructed upon a false foundation of insecurity and fear.

I come to you to remind you that Upheaval is a disruption that is needed to break the wall down between your ego and your soul, and illuminate the false idea of your identity and worth. Built from fear, control, false security, collective experiences and beliefs. I remind you that shock, loss, and collapsing beliefs and endeavors will cause you to expand beyond the walls of your ego and open to your true self as a spiritual being living a human experience. The ego is not the enemy, it just needs to realize who is the captain of the ship. This captain, with a compassionate heart, coaxes the ego into its proper job of copilot, navigating alongside the soul, knowing it must let go of control to survive the storm. There is little you can do but let the illusions, control, old beliefs, and walls crumble, for crisis clears the way for the soul to expand and illuminate your truth and life. This upheaval is powerful, a tremendous release into a new direction of true freedom. Have faith, there will be peace after the storm.

Astrological Planets:

Uranus: *The Rebel Liberator (Rules Aquarius):* Sudden change, seeking freedom in the unknown, breakthroughs, rebirth, genius, inventor, rebel, originality, individuality, sudden change, the awakener**,** unpredictable, shocking, out of the blue, crisis.

Saturn: *The Titan of Trade, Wealth, Agriculture, Work Ethic, and Time. (Rules Capricorn & Aquarius):* Margins, boundaries, accountability, restriction, structure, successful business, responsibilities, commitments, self-control, personal limits, self-empowerment, leadership, harvest, time management, cold, aloof miserly, strict, obstinate, calculating, unfriendly.

Pluto: *The Magician of Empowerment and Transformation (Rules Scorpio)* Death and regeneration, power, control, rebirth, letting go, destruction, profound change, dark night of the soul, surrender, catharsis, emotional release, purification, personal transformation, intense power.

Mars: *The Valiant Warrior (Rules Aries & Scorpio):* Active, courage, strength, building, force, energy, leadership, pushing forward, warrior, aggressive, reactive, competitive, combative, conflict, controlling, violence.

Astrological Signs:

Aries (Fire): *The Warrior of Power:* Illuminating, consciousness, expressing, energy, activating, essence, vitality, identity, creating, initiating, headstrong, aggressive, risk-taking, rash, impulsive, competitive, egotistical, dominating, pushy, selfish, conflictive.

Aquarius (Air): *The Cosmic Intuitive Genius:* Open, progressive, vast, remarkable, intelligent, original, restructuring, sovereign, peculiar, liberal, inventive, drastic, outrageous, erratic, detached, obstinate, scandalous, spacey, weird, troublemaking, mechanized, impulsive, fanatical, unreasonable, mutinous, inflexible.

Scorpio (Water): *The Powerful Mysterious Psychic*: Powerful, intense, passionate, inquisitive, magnetic, deep, fierce, mysterious, psychic, esoteric, cryptic, sexy, seductive, faithful, secretive, mesmerizing, envious, magical, observant, obsessive, dark, calculating, compulsive, complicated, jealous, irritable.

Capricorn (Earth): *The Proficient Leader:* Utilizing, practical, concrete, efficient, patient with restrictions, overcoming obstacles, climbing to the top, natural, leadership, aloof, unpractical, impatient, unorganized controlling, bossy, harsh, tyrannical.

Numerological Vibration: 16

1. One: Beginnings, independence, creation, foundation of everything, natural born leader, pioneering spirit, uniqueness, motivational, full of energy, vitality, leadership, follower, unmotivated, codependent, apathetic, uninterested, lazy.

6. Six: Harmonic love, magnetic, understanding, compassionate, balanced, nurturing, family, home, affectionate, loving, dependable, reliable, care taker, provider, serving loved ones, self-righteous, critical, people pleasing, negligent, intrusive, nosy, overprotective, unstable.

(The Total Numerological Vibration is 7)

7. Seven: Sees the underlying meaning and truth of realities, philosopher, the sage, the seeker of truth, the intellectual, healer, spiritual, psychic, hidden illusions, faith, introspection, spiritual awaking, inner-knowing, the esoteric, negative, rigidity, gloominess, doubtful.

Symbolism:

Brick Wall: Wounded ego, false self, lower mind, beliefs, motives, fabrications, closed off, defensive.

Screaming (Defense Alarms): Anger, crisis, reactionary, wounded ego, emotions.

Mirror Image: Shadow, ego self.

Eye: True self-awareness, spiritual self, soul, higher-self, clarity, light, new vision, new-self, openness, cycles.

17. The Star

"Always be yourself, express yourself, have faith in yourself." - Bruce Lee

Affirmations:
I trust, I inspire, I create, I shine, I believe, I guide, I succeed, I motivate.

Key Words:
Light at the end of the tunnel, inspiration, guidance, creativity, trust, hope, faith, prosperity, believing, blessings, great expectations, gratitude, astrological arts, motivation, inner strength, receiving answers, love flowing freely, open heart, stillness, calm, relaxed, untroubled, clear vision, clear guidance, uplifting.

Description:
The Star rests peacefully adorned with eight points of her celestial crown embraced by the mountain of earth and carried by the waters of the ocean. She holds her hands to her chest feeling the love and faith from within her heart that she is supported and loved by the creative source, to shine brightly for all those who seek guidance and help. Through light, gratitude, and an open heart she sends inspiration, peace, and faith to all those in need of support and hope along the journey of life.

Guidance:
I am The Star. I represent trust, faith, and creativity. I am the twinkling light that guides your heart. I am the faith that illuminates your path and the trust that saturates your being. I bring promise of peace and creativity. I assist the release of pain, fear, and struggle from your heart and urge you to trust and allow healing of oneself by following the illumination of The Star.
I come to you to share faith, trust, and hope of a bright future. I remind you to maintain belief in the light that glows within you. I guide you with inspiration, clarity of purpose, and a wonderful new start of auspicious opportunities. I spark imagination, ambition, success, and energy to make your dreams a reality. Have faith, connect with your inner star. You will never be led astray by the light, for you are a magnificent being worthy of knowing everything will work out for your highest and greatest good.

Astrological Planets:

Jupiter: *The Teacher of Expansion and Luck (Rules Sagittarius):* Faith, hope, spiritual and intellectual exploration, higher learning, abstract thinking, religion, philosophy, moral and ethical values, expansion, opportunist, snobbish, egotistical, condescending, cruel, and off-putting.

Uranus: *The Rebel Liberator (Rules Aquarius):* Sudden change, seeking freedom in the unknown, breakthroughs, rebirth, genius, inventor, rebel, originality, individuality, sudden change, the awakener, unpredictable, shocking, out of the blue, crisis.

Neptune: *The Channel of Divine Union* (*Rules Pisces)* Spirituality, tranquility, happiness, peace, kindness, mind's eye, intuition, compassion, creation, imagination, magic, miracles, connection, unity, merging, nebulous, mystery, boundless mysticism, letting go, atonement, faith, home, supported, loved, relaxed, illusion, self-deception, escapism, drugs, self-undoing, self-deception, confusion, weakness, self-imprisonment.

Astrological Signs:

Aquarius (Air): *The Cosmic Intuitive Genius:* Open, progressive, vast, remarkable, intelligent, original, restructuring, sovereign, peculiar, liberal, inventive, drastic, outrageous, erratic, detached, obstinate, scandalous, spacey, weird, troublemaking, mechanized, impulsive, fanatical, unreasonable, mutinous, inflexible.

Sagittarius (Fire): *The Free-Spirited Adventurer*: Ambitious, positive, optimist, wit, sincere, clear-cut, spur-of-the-moment, enthusiastic, thoughtful, philosophical, candid, open-minded, edification, publishing, tactless, domineering, arrogant, fanatical, dogmatic, patronizing, unbalanced ego, rambling, careless, irresponsible, restless, aloof, emotionally detached.

Cancer (Water): *The Empathic Healer:* Energy, tides, ebb and flow, cycles, movement, water, moon, mother intuitive, nurturing, family, home, supportive, provides safety, comfort and foresight, anxious, emotionally attached to the past, touchy, defensive, co-dependent, self-doubting, unstable, high and mighty, afraid, withdrawn, frantic, calculating.

Numerological Vibration: 17

1. One: Beginnings, independence, creation, foundation of everything, natural born leader, pioneering spirit, uniqueness, motivational, full of energy, vitality, leadership, follower, unmotivated, codependent, apathetic, uninterested, lazy.

7. Seven: Sees the underlying meaning and truth of realities, philosopher, the sage, the seeker of truth, the intellectual, healer, spiritual, psychic, hidden illusions, faith, introspection, spiritual awaking, inner-knowing, the esoteric, negative, rigidity, gloominess, doubtful.

(The Total Numerological Vibration is 8)

8. Eight: Abundance, material attainment, dependable, efficient, accomplishment, ambition, building useful things for the world, successful management, flourishing, reality, practical, courage, material success, problem solving, organization, impractical, stubborn, lacking ambition, unorganized.

Symbolism:

Mountains: Earth, boundaries, structure, adventure, stability, conquering and overcoming obstacles, the journey ahead, grounding self, rough terrain, challenges.

Star Crown: Crown chakra, unified emotional and mental intelligence, positivity, faith, hope, trust, inspiration, light, abundance, self-reliance, energy, guidance, intuition, solitude, peace, astrology, and creativity.

Vale/Ocean: Water and earth emotions, openness through grounding and support.

Hand over Heart: Love, creativity, faith, giving, receiving, heart consciousness, believing, and gratitude.

18. The Moon

"Three things cannot be long hidden: the sun, the moon, and the truth." - Buddha

Affirmations:
I enchant, I mystify, I dream, I deceive, I confuse, I feel, I wax and wane.

Key Words:
Subconscious and unconscious mind, dreams, psychic messages, intuition, shadow-self, guidance, crisis of faith, illusions, confusion, empathy, projection doubt, and self-imposed limitations.

Description:
The mystical moon roams the vast terrain of the subconscious mind. The guardian of the mysterious empire of light and dark, ebb and flow, waxing and waning, projecting instincts and reactions, as well as evoking and nourishing the empathic dreamer of the psychic tides of the unconscious sea.

Guidance:
I am The Moon. I represent the unconscious realm of the unknown, a deep intuitive magic, the psychic dream world, illusions, and the dwelling of the shadow self. I symbolize unconscious emotion and core beliefs hidden in the shadows, waiting to be illuminated by the light of the sun. I inspire the urge of internal desire and emotional needs. I bring self-imposed confusion and a crisis of faith, yet emotionally guide you to your intuition and dreams, which hold messages and keys to the doors of your expanded consciousness.

I come to help you trust your feelings and to look within your unconscious for answers. I remind you the moonlight can be deceptive so examine your motives and those of others while faced with dilemmas and doubt. I will help guide you by speaking to you through your emotional intelligence. I assist in uncovering all that seeks to be illuminated in the empire of the captivating unknown, where dreams, fear, and imagination live side by side. I advise you to be aware of the illusions coming forth from the dark side of the moon for not everything is as it seems in the kingdom of the unknown.

Astrological Planets:

Moon: *The Empath of The Subconscious Ocean (Rules Cancer)*: Water, intuition, tides, ebb and flow, feminine, subconscious, reactions, instinct, basic habits, personal needs, co-dependent, inconsistent, easily set off, reactive, overly emotional, depressed, mood swings.

Neptune: *The Channel of Divine Union* (*Rules Pisces*) Spirituality, tranquility, happiness, peace, kindness, mind's eye, intuition, compassion, creation, imagination, magic, miracles, connection, unity, merging, nebulous, mystery, boundless mysticism, letting go, atonement, faith, home, supported, loved, relaxed, illusion, self-deception, escapism, drugs, self-undoing, self-deception, confusion, weakness, self-imprisonment.

Astrological Signs:

Cancer (Water): *The Empathic Healer:* Energy, tides, ebb and flow, cycles, movement, water, moon, mother intuitive, nurturing, family, home, supportive, provides safety, comfort and foresight, anxious, emotionally attached to the past, touchy, defensive, co-dependent, self-doubting, unstable, high and mighty, afraid, withdrawn, frantic, calculating.

Scorpio (Water): *The Powerful Mysterious Psychic*: Powerful, intense, passionate, inquisitive, magnetic, deep, fierce, mysterious, psychic, esoteric, cryptic, sexy, seductive, faithful, secretive, mesmerizing, envious, magical, observant, obsessive, dark, calculating, compulsive, complicated, jealous, irritable.

Pisces (Water): *The Mystical Visionary:* The soul, third eye, visions, spirituality, dreams, imagination, feelings, impressions, vulnerability, compassion, water, ocean, visionary artist, intuitive, mystic, oracle, psychic, poet, musician, dreamer, spacey, evasive, escapist, vague, abused, deceptive, depressed, foggy, illusory, delusional, passive, confused.

Numerological Vibration: 18

1. One: Beginnings, independence, creation, foundation of everything, natural born leader, pioneering spirit, uniqueness, motivational, full of energy, vitality, leadership, follower, unmotivated, codependent, apathetic, uninterested, lazy.

8. Eight: Abundance, material attainment, dependable, efficient, accomplishment, ambition, building useful things for the world, successful management, flourishing, reality, practical, courage, material success, problem solving, organization, impractical, stubborn, lacking ambition, unorganized.

(The Total Numerological Vibration is 9)

9. Nine: Universal energies, inner wisdom, responsibility, service to humanity, compassion, selflessness, protective energy, love of nature and earth, light working, service, benevolent, selfless, advanced souls, stressed, uptight, trying to solve everyone's problems, willing victim, overbearing, dogmatic, self-righteous.

Symbolism:

Androgynous Figure Both female and male intuition.

Seed of Life Pattern: Symbolic of creation, dreams, unconscious, and projection.

Star Pattern on Robe: Faith, creativity, dreams, hope, guidance, the cosmos, and astrology.

Mountains: Earth, boundaries, structure, adventure, stability, conquering and overcoming obstacles, the journey ahead, grounding self, rough terrain, challenges.

Crescent Moon (Represents both Waxing and Waning):

Waxing Moon: Growth, manifestation, attainment. Waxing moon is the movement of the new moon increasing in light towards the full moon

Waning Moon: Letting go, contemplation. Waning moon is the movement of the full moon decreasing in light towards the new moon.

19. The Sun

"We all shine on, like the moon, and the stars, and the sun." - John Lennon

Affirmations:
I illuminate, I shine, I appreciate, I play, I expand, I radiate.

Key Words:
New level of insight shining on all that is hidden, clarity, illumination, enlightened, greatness, success, happiness, vitality, growth, love, sunshine, play, rest, warmth, carefree, energizing, joy, health, freedom, expansive, honoring self, confidence, self-worth, self-trust, vibrant energy, healthy ego.

Description:
The Sun smiles with radiant love illuminating her path with clarity, joy and vitality. Her hands rise in play for she is in love with her own light which increases as she basks in her growing energy and warmth.

Guidance:
I am The Sun. I represent energy and light, growth and warmth. I am the soul and true self illuminated. I succeed in shining my light as I know my true value and self-worth. I am brilliant, and I radiate light from within which shines in the outer world. My vitality radiates for all who are within my gaze for I am the light in the darkness. I am the expansive energy that grows beyond limitations and I represent the soul energy within your being bursting with valiant rays of love and light.
I come to you to illuminate your path and to help you remember your own brilliant light. You are magnificent, beautiful, and worthy of shining your unique light for all to see. Go forth on your path with confidence joy and love. Your light is needed not only for you but for those who may be afraid to shine themselves. Your joyful example will spread light to many and help illuminate the darkness, but most importantly, shine for yourself.

Astrological Planet:
Sun: *The Illuminator of Life (Rules Leo):* Illumination, warmth, vitality, success, happiness, light, honors, personal power, expression, empowerment, intense, burning, and overpowering.

Astrological Sign:

Leo (Fire): *The Sovereign Performer:* Sovereignty, rulership, courage, self-expression, self-appreciation, playful, kind, open, welcoming, considerate, warm, reliable, energetic, unkind, callous, unreceptive, arrogant, blocked, insensitive, undependable.

Numerological Vibration: 19

1. One: Beginnings, independence, creation, foundation of everything, natural born leader, pioneering spirit, uniqueness, motivational, full of energy, vitality, leadership, follower, unmotivated, codependent, apathetic, uninterested, lazy.

9. Nine: Universal energies, inner wisdom, responsibility, service to humanity, compassion, selflessness, protective energy, love of nature and earth, light working, service, benevolent, selfless, advanced souls, stressed, uptight, trying to solve everyone's problems, willing victim, overbearing, dogmatic, self-righteous.

(The Total Numerological Vibration is 10)

1. One: Beginnings, independence, creation, foundation of everything, natural born leader, pioneering spirit, uniqueness, motivational, full of energy, vitality, leadership, follower, unmotivated, codependent, apathetic, uninterested, lazy.

0. Zero: The source of all numbers, increases value of other numbers, male and female, alpha & omega, everything and nothing, potential and choice.

Symbolism:

Female Figure: The Sun is traditionally represented as male, yet the female Sun represents a shift of balance of male and female energies occurring on earth.

Mountains: Earth, boundaries, structure, adventure, stability, conquering and overcoming obstacles, the journey ahead, grounding self, rough terrain, challenges.

Hands Up: Carefree, self-love, self-appreciation.

Head Dress: The unique energy patterns of light in all of us individually.

Full Skirt: Expansive, fullness of life, beauty, protection.

Rays of Light: Light, love, energy, vitality.

20. Awakening

"This above all; to your own self be true." - *William Shakespeare*

Affirmations:

I awaken, I stand in my truth, I answer the call within, I release the past, I forgive.

Key Words:

Awakening, revelation, rebirth, inner calling, taking a stand, awakening to possibilities, truth, seeing things in a new light, significant life change, reviewing past actions, rite of passage, renewed hope, answering the call within, true vocation, inner convictions, conclusions, rewards, second chances, making a difference, releasing guilt, releasing sorrow, forgiveness of self and others, reconciliation with past, balanced judgments, reinvention, success.

Description:

The awakened one stands in her power, claiming her divine sovereign higher mind. A declaration of her internal truth, a long-awaited shift, a new beginning, and an ending of her old life that was a falsehood masking her sight. This claiming of free will is a second chance to reinvent herself for her highest good and to fulfill her potential as a spirit experiencing itself as a human being.

Guidance:

I am Awakening. I represent the energy of awakening to the inner call of reinventing the union of the spiritual self. I am second chances reviewing hindsight and experiences. I am rewarded with rebirth of new vision and life. I am the guardian of resurrection. I awaken to my true calling with renewed hope and faith. I release guilt and sorrow. I forgive the past, for it brought this beautiful rite of passage, illuminating inner knowing, endless love, self-empowerment and infinite possibilities.

I come to remind you to awaken to hope and absolution. To forgive yourself and others and release the past. To awaken to a fresh perspective of self. You have come far, and this second chance gives insight and awakening with the benefits of wisdom and retrospection. Let all past hurts go so you can have peace and conclusion before you reinvent yourself. Open your eyes, open your heart, and rebirth a new self. Go forth and allow the radiant true self to manifest. Be open to receiving the beautiful discovery of your highest self. You are sure to succeed on your path.

Astrological Planets:

Sun: *The Illuminator of Life (Rules Leo):* Illumination, warmth, vitality, success, happiness, light, honors, personal power, expression, empowerment, intense, burning, and overpowering.

Uranus: *The Rebel Liberator (Rules Aquarius):* Sudden change, seeking freedom in the unknown, breakthroughs, rebirth, genius, inventor, rebel, originality, individuality, sudden change, the awakener, unpredictable, shocking, out of the blue, crisis.

Pluto: *The Magician of Empowerment and Transformation (Rules Scorpio)* Death and regeneration, power, control, rebirth, letting go, destruction, profound change, dark night of the soul, surrender, catharsis, emotional release, purification, personal transformation, intense power.

Astrological Signs:

Aquarius (Air): *The Cosmic Intuitive Genius:* Open, progressive, vast, remarkable, intelligent, original, restructuring, sovereign, peculiar, liberal, inventive, drastic, outrageous, erratic, detached, obstinate, scandalous, spacey, weird, troublemaking, mechanized, impulsive, fanatical, unreasonable, mutinous, inflexible.

Pisces (Water): *The Mystical Visionary:* The soul, third eye, visions, spirituality, dreams, imagination, feelings, impressions, vulnerability, compassion, water, ocean, visionary artist, intuitive, mystic, oracle, psychic, poet, musician, dreamer, spacey, evasive, escapist, vague, abused, deceptive, depressed, foggy, illusory, delusional, passive, confused.

Aries (Fire): *The Warrior of Power:* Illuminating, consciousness, expressing, energy, activating, essence, vitality, identity, creating, initiating, headstrong, aggressive, risk-taking, rash, impulsive, competitive, egotistical, dominating, pushy, selfish, conflictive.

Numerological Vibration: 20

2. Two: Unity, balance, polarity, diplomatic, service, compassion, nurturing, marriage, co-operation, adaptability, mirroring, relationships, unstable, unbalanced, disturbed, unhinged, one-sided, codependent, coldness.

0. Zero: The source of all numbers, increases value of other numbers, male and female, alpha & omega, everything and nothing, potential and choice.

(The Total Numerological Vibration is 2)

2. Two: Unity, balance, polarity, diplomatic, service, compassion, nurturing, marriage, co-operation, adaptability, mirroring, relationships, unstable, unbalanced, disturbed, unhinged, one-sided, codependent, coldness.

Symbolism:

The Awakened One: Empowered self, the true self within the soul, the lower mind merging with the higher mind.

Roses: Growth, balance, promise, flowering consciousness, hope, new beginnings, love, honor.

Right Hand: Personal power, strength, human action aligned with thought, being aware of physical and emotional intelligence.

The Eye: Awakening, third eye, presence, observation, awareness, opening, gateway of infinite intelligence, and expansion.

21. Wholeness

"You are the universe, you aren't in the universe." - Eckhart Tolle

Affirmations:

I exist, I accomplish, I complete, I succeed, I flourish, I give and receive, I choose, I Integrate, I expand, I create, I am whole.

Key Words:

Existence, wholeness, the world, fulfillment, the universe, integration, accomplishment, involvement, field of conscious energy, prosperity, heart's desire, dream come true, flourishing, expansion, beautiful solutions, abundance, choices, contribution, healing, service, gifts and talents, sharing, giving, receiving, fulfillment, pleasure in life, peace, satisfaction, counting blessings, gratitude, harmony, fruits, rewards, celebration, success.

Description:

Within the fabric of existence appears vortices of consciousness that dance in the universal field of infinite awareness and expanding life. The hands of the divine human who has completed their passage of awakening reach within, and blissfully select from all the blossoming gifts that are presented for a job well done.

Guidance:

We are Wholeness. We represent the energy of the undivided totality of all that is. We are the field of infinite intelligence. We represent completion and achievement, fulfillment of dreams, unified intention, and the heart's desire. We represent all beautiful solutions, consciousness, rewards, and peaceful integration. We bestow energy and the fruits of human contribution to the world and the universe. We are opportunity and the source of true inner joy and satisfaction. We are unlimited, we are absolute, we are whole.

We come to you to remind you that you have the universe within you and the world within your hands. You are completely whole and are rewarded for all your accomplishments and service to the highest good of yourself and the assistance given to others in love. You have achieved a great deal of success along your journey and have overcome many obstacles while holding faith in the darkest of hours. We present abundance, fulfillment, and peace. Now is the time to reap your rewards for a job well done! Go forth and choose from the infinite gifts available to you. The difficulties of the past are behind you. Celebrate your triumphs and accept applause, for you have completed a major life cycle and all has come full circle.

Astrological Planets:

Neptune: *The Channel of Divine Union* (***Rules Pisces)*** Spirituality, tranquility, happiness, peace, kindness, mind's eye, intuition, compassion, creation, imagination, magic, miracles, connection, unity, merging, nebulous, mystery, boundless mysticism, letting go, atonement, faith, home, supported, loved, relaxed, illusion, self-deception, escapism, drugs, self-undoing, self-deception, confusion, weakness, self-imprisonment.

Earth: *The Mother of Nourishment and Growth*: Creative, beautiful, patient, hardworking, practical, grounded, abundant, form, physical, variety, focused, supportive, structure, the four elements - fire, water, air, and earth, stability, protection, harvest, ungrounded, stubborn, unstable, lack, impatient, unfocused, apathetic, destructive, lazy.

Astrological Signs:

Aires, Taurus, Gemini, Cancer, Leo, Virgo, Libra, Scorpio, Sagittarius, Capricorn, Aquarius, Pisces.

Numerological Vibration: 21

2. Two: Unity, balance, polarity, diplomatic, service, compassion, nurturing, marriage, co-operation, adaptability, mirroring, relationships, unstable, unbalanced, disturbed, unhinged, one-sided, codependent, coldness.

1. One: Beginnings, independence, creation, foundation of everything, natural born leader, pioneering spirit, uniqueness, motivational, full of energy, vitality, leadership, follower, unmotivated, codependent, apathetic, uninterested, lazy.

(The Total Numerological Vibration is 3)

3. Three: Creativity, inspiration, self-expression, joy, triad, catalyst, trinity, manifestation, growth, multiplicity, beginning-middle-end, pyramid, triangle.

Symbolism:

Hands Right and Left: Wholeness in the physical as well as spiritual, the universe is within, the world is in your hands, stability, accomplishment, a choice of abundant rewards, integration, service.

The Circles: Gateways, vortices, flowering, wholeness and totality.

Eyes: Omnipresence, intelligence, light, transcendental view of life and consciousness.

Vines: Growth, fruits, rewards, opportunity, regeneration, connection, fertility, expansion and bounty.

Meditative & Trance Coloring

I created twenty-two patterns for meditative trance coloring to complement the twenty-two archetypes that inspire spiritual creative experiences.

Coloring repetitive patterns can induce a trance-like state. Trances are a half-conscious state, seemingly between sleeping and waking like a dream. Similar to various meditative states of consciousness.

Meditation is defined as a practice where an individual focuses his or her mind on an item, thought, or activity to achieve a mentally clear and emotionally calm state. Meditation and trance coloring may be used to reduce stress, anxiety, depression, and pain.

Personally, in this state of being, I experience profound mystical experiences while engaged in a creative rhythmic action especially creating and coloring repetitive shapes and patterns. I also experience many epiphanies, revelations, recollections of forgotten memories within the subconscious, mindful reflection, and ease of emotional and physical pain.

Much love, may your visions be meditative as well as illuminated.

Julia Luke

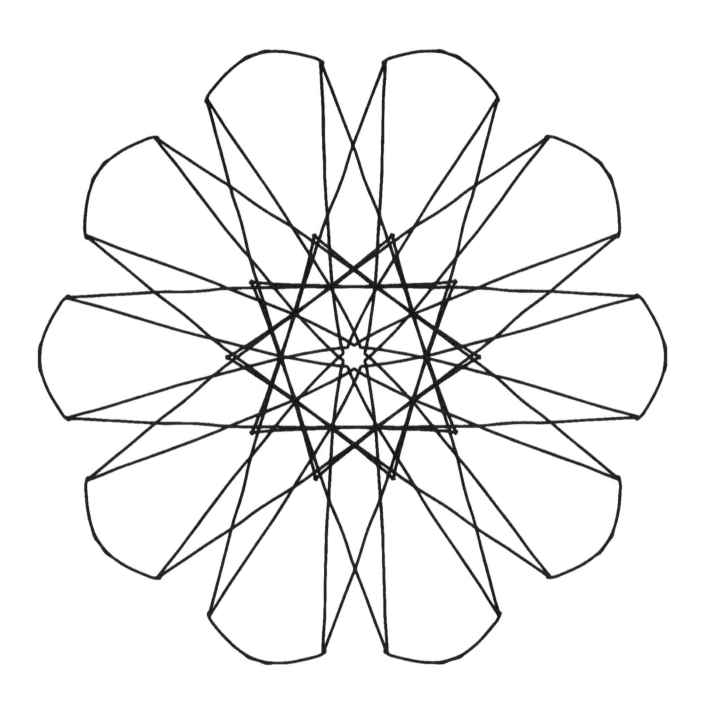

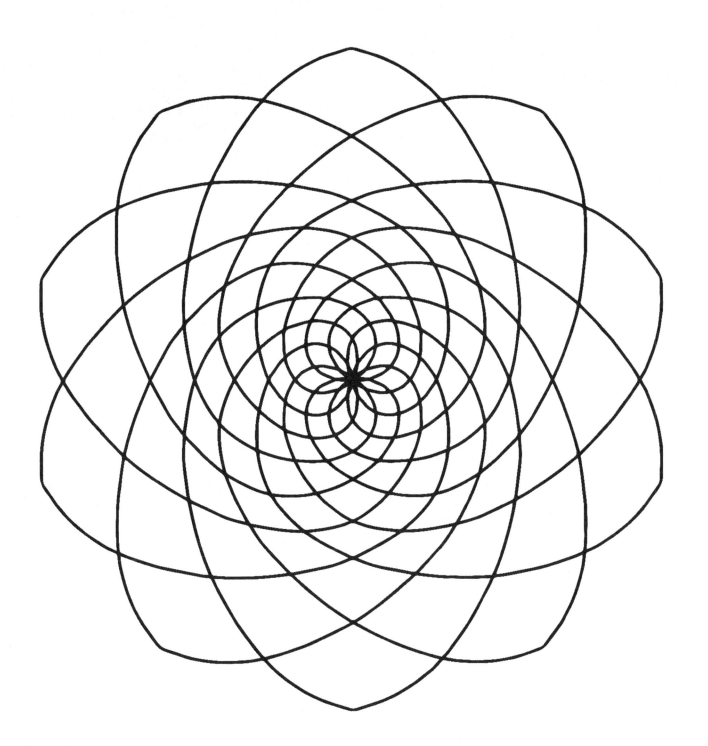

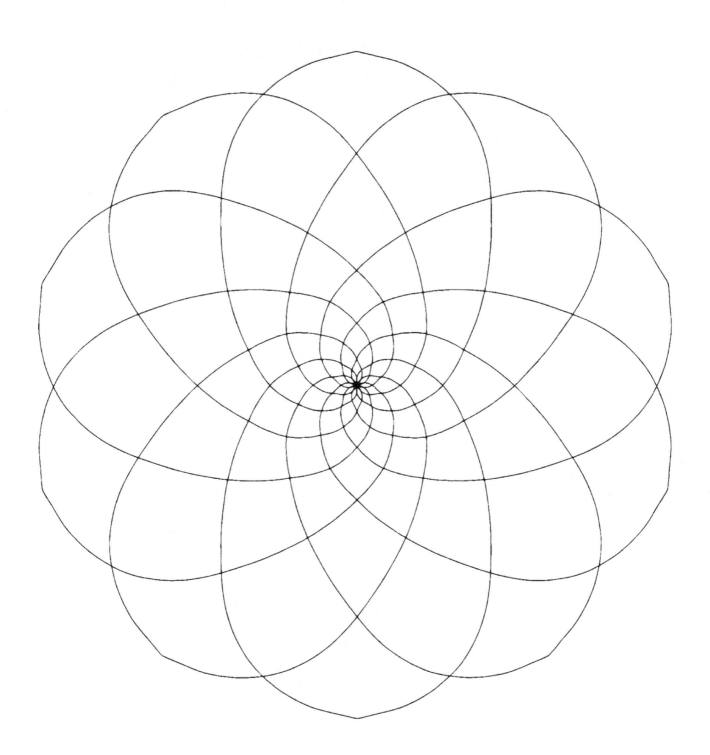

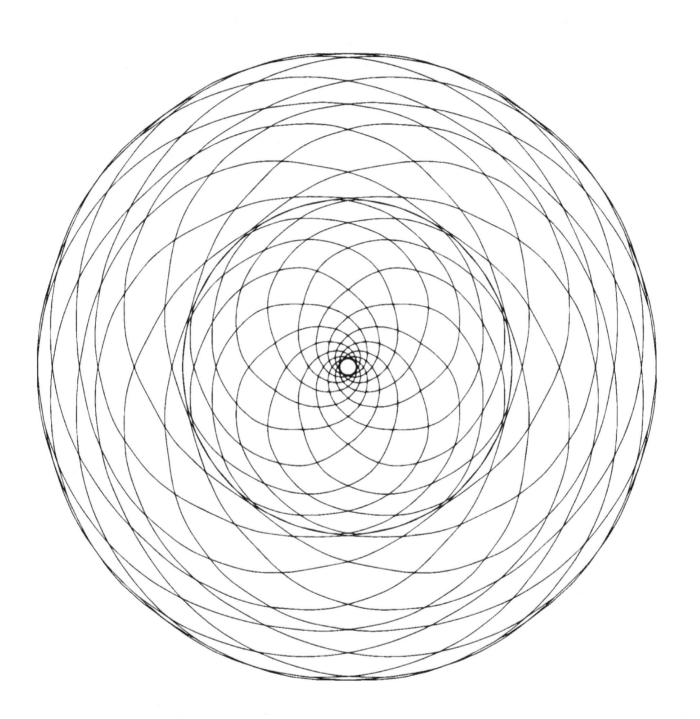

Made in the USA
Monee, IL
12 January 2020